THE MOST INCREDIBLE HUNTING STORIES EVER TOLD

TRUE TALES ABOUT HUNTING, TRAPPING, ADVENTURE AND SURVIVAL

JONATHAN HUNT

ISBN: 979-8-89095-008-6

CONTENTS

ATTENTION:

DO YOU WANT MY FUTURE BOOKS AT HEAVY DISCOUNTS AND EVEN FOR FREE?

HEAD OVER TO WWW.SECRETREADS.COM AND JOIN MY SECRET BOOK CLUB!

INTRODUCTION

Imagine being mauled by a bear while alone in the woods. Or being attacked by a pack of wild dogs. Or being dragged underwater by a shark with its jaws locked around your leg. Or being stranded for a week in the mountains of Alaska. Or stranded for a month in the jungles of the Amazon.

If you were a hunter who found yourself in any of the above situations, to what lengths would you go to survive?

This is the exact question that real-life hunters have had to ask themselves when they find themselves right in those same situations.

Every one of these hunters survived thanks to deploying just the right combination of willpower and intelligence..., and maybe a little bit of luck.

Part of the thrill of hunting is the risk that is always involved. Yes, there's always the thrill of the hunt and guessing whether or not the hunt will be successful, and the thrill of the chase once you've found or detected your prey.

But there's also the inherent risk of finding yourself stranded alone in the wilderness or being viciously attacked by a dangerous wild animal with no one else there to help you.

If you do ever find yourself in a life-or-death situation on a future hunting trip, you'll be forced to do whatever it takes to make it out alive. Reading the real-life stories of other hunters who found themselves in such situations and learning from them is critical.

That's because, if you ever find yourself in a similar situation, you can do what they did, and this could be what ultimately saves your life.

In this book, we'll tell the true stories of hunters who soon found themselves in a life-or-death battle for survival. We'll talk about the circumstances that led up to these events, how they made it out alive, and what they did to recover from it.

Every one of these stories actually happened, and they each have a valuable lesson (or multiple lessons) to learn about survival.

Let's get started.

CHAPTER ONE

CALM AND COLLECTED

An elk hunter known for his very calm demeanor had his composure challenged, to say the least, when he was confronted by a grizzly bear on one of his hunting trips in the mountains of Wyoming. This is his story.

Jeremy Dickson was always known for his calm yet confident disposition.

A graduate of Lovell High School in 1995, Dickson grew up in the Wyoming backcountry and always fitted the classic profile of the quiet, relaxed, and yet rugged outdoorsman.

Located right in the middle of the Rockies, Wyoming is noted for its towering mountains, sprawling Douglas fir forests, flowing streams and rivers, and abundance of wildlife. In the fall, Wyoming is any hunter's heaven.

It was early October of 2021, during elk hunting season in the region. Dickson, along with three of his hunting buddies, embarked on what was supposed to be another ordinary elk hunting trip on Grizzly Ridge, near the small Wyoming town of Wapiti.

The word 'Wapiti' is the Cree Indian name for elk. So, it was apt that Dickson would go elk hunting in the area.

The party of four headed out into the hunting grounds. Dickson was well aware of the threat of grizzlies in the area. After all, the area they were hunting in was called Grizzly Ridge. Dickson had observed grizzly bears often, albeit from a distance, on numerous occasions when hunting in the region.

That's why besides his .300 Magnum bolt action hunting rifle, Dickson always carried a 10mm Auto handgun when he ventured out into Grizzly Ridge.

The 10mm is a good round for self-defense against wild big game animals because it offers good stopping power and ballistics roughly equivalent to that of a .357 Magnum revolver, and yet as a semi-automatic pistol has greater capacity in the magazine and a faster reloading time (if necessary). Dickson never ventured out to Grizzly Ridge unprepared.

The first day of the hunt for Dickson and his hunting buddies was a success. They downed an elk and were all eager to continue the hunt the next day.

But Dickson was also acutely aware that downing an elk usually attracted predators and scavengers - including bears.

That's why when they got up early the next morning to continue the hunt on horseback, the group of four hunters were actively looking for bears as a precaution.

Dickson recalls, "One of the other guys had shot an elk [the day before], and before we took off down there, we told him, "remember where that elk was down there and pay attention about the bears." We knew there'd be one somewhere. We all knew to pay attention because we thought there'd be one around."

Ascending a hill on their horses, Dickson and one of his hunting partners, John, dismounted and continued on foot for roughly 200 yards. It was then that they spotted elk on the other side of the ridge.

Dickson pulled out a pair of binoculars to observe the elk.

That was when, in this one moment that he wasn't actively looking around him for signs of bears, a bear appeared.

"She came over the top from the east side of the ridge about 15 to 20 yards away from us," Dickson recalls. "We were looking at the elk, and she came from behind us. And when she got about three or four yards away from us, that's when she started making some noise. It's kind of crazy. It actually sounded like a pig, kind of a squeal, not as high pitched, but that's what it reminded me of, a pig."

Imagine finding yourself in that situation, where you're looking through binoculars at something far away and are fully focused on what you're seeing when suddenly you hear those noises just as Dickson described.

By then, it was too late for Dickson to react. The bear was only roughly fifteen yards away, but it closed in fast. Bears are animals of both great power and speed, and now Dickson was on the receiving end of this ferocious animal that had every intent to kill him without delay.

As Dickson turned to the noise and spotted the bear charging him head-on, his hand instinctively moved for that 10mm pistol he always carried in his chest rig. Before he could get the gun out of his holster, the mighty bear was already over him.

The animal knocked Dickson down to the ground. Dickson instinctively raised his left arm to defend himself, and the bear's powerful jaws clamped over his lower hand. Its teeth pierced through bone and flesh.

As Dickson wrestled with the massive beast, his partner John reacted instinctively. John raised his .300 Magnum rifle to his shoulder and fired the moment the butt of the gun reached his shoulder.

The big round struck the bear in the shoulder, causing it to wheel around and confront John, who was rechambering his rifle to take another shot. In the process, the bear released its grip over Dickson's hand.

Though his left hand was nearly useless, Dickson managed to get up while drawing his 10mm out of its holster with his right hand.

As the bear prepared to charge John as it had Dickson, he fired multiple rounds at the animal at close range.

Already mortally wounded from the rifle shot, the bear dropped to the ground as the pistol rounds struck. Dickson continued to fire a couple of more shots into the now motionless body to confirm the bear was dead and could do no more.

And just like that, the battle was over.

Attempting to catch his breath, Dickson realized the damage the animal had done to him. His left thumb had been ripped from its socket and was now hanging from his hand with just flesh and skin.

It was then that Dickson realized that even though the battle with the grizzly was over, the struggle to survive was not.

As mentioned before, Dickson was known by his friends and family throughout his life for his calm and collected demeanor. He was naturally analytic, and even though his heart was pounding, and his adrenaline was rushing from the encounter, these core traits did not abandon him.

Immediately, Dickson got to thinking about the actions he and John would need to take next.

The first thing they did was contact their two other hunting buddies, who were a few hundred yards away on the same ridge. Getting through to them via radio, which is commonly used by hunters for communication in the mountains due to the lack of cell or internet service, they rapidly explained what had happened and requested them to bring down the horses.

While waiting for their hunting friends to return, Dickson and John fashioned a tourniquet to stop the flow of blood out of Dickson's hand. They then covered Dickson's entire hand with a wool sock to keep it covered from the elements and reduce the chance of a deadly infection setting in.

Their two friends with the horses appeared just as Dickson and John had finished fashioning the makeshift bandage. Mounting the animals, the hunters rode down the hill to their camp and got in contact with emergency medical professionals. They were told that the nearest helicopter would be two to three hours away.

They continued to ride their horses down to the North Fork Highway, which was about the same time away as the helicopter would be. It was during this ride that Dickson called his wife,

Carmen, to inform her of the incident and to tell her to meet him at the hospital.

Carmen noted that Dickson was already making light of the situation when he called her.

"My thumb is just along for the ride," she recalls him saying. She knew that her husband's usual sense of humor meant he was going to be okay.

The foursome then arrived at the North Fork, where a helicopter was indeed waiting for Dickson in the parking area.

Climbing into the helicopter, Dickson was received by the medical professionals waiting inside. The helicopter then carried them to the nearest hospital.

* * *

At the hospital, Dickson learned the extent of his injuries. While he suffered no broken bones, the bear had literally ripped his thumb out of its socket. Thankfully, the tourniquet he and John had fashioned had kept the thumb in place and saved it.

Another miracle was the fact that the surgeon at the hospital happened to be an orthopedic hand surgeon by the name of Barry Smith. He even had prior experience in dealing with injuries to the hand from bear attacks! It may have been Dickson and John's tourniquet that saved Dickson's thumb immediately following the attack, but it was Smith's successful surgical operation afterwards that ensured Dickson would keep and use his thumb as normal for the rest of his life.

At the end of the day, everything following the attack worked out in Dickson's favor. He fashioned a tourniquet that saved his thumb, he was able to get in contact with his wife and explain the situation, the horses did not cause any problems on the ride back, and he and his hunting friends made it back to the end of the trail just when the helicopter arrived.

In other words, Dickson applied first aid, stayed calm, and made it back to civilization. And at the end of all of it, the surgeon who treated Dickson's injuries ended up being specifically suited to the task.

Two days later, Dickson was out of the hospital, and later in the week, he was back to work. His thumb was extremely uncomfortable for some time after the incident, but he continued to recover fast and regained the use of it.

The core lesson of Dickson's story is clear: when you're attacked by a wild animal while out in the woods, stay calm and collected in order to make it out alive.

Dickson, with the aid of his friend John, was able to successfully defend himself against the bear and immediately apply first aid and get to work on making it back to civilization alive. He was only able to achieve this by staying calm and thinking carefully and decisively enough to take the necessary actions that resulted in his survival.

Today, Jeremy Dickson is still hunting.

CHAPTER TWO

ALWAYS WEAR YOUR LIFE VEST

A trio of duck hunters found out the hard way to always wear a life vest when you go bird hunting in a boat…especially in the frigid waters of a Minnesota lake.

Minnesota is a state known as the 'Land of 10,000 Lakes'.

Actually, that's a little bit of an understatement. The reality is that Minnesota boasts 14,000 lakes scattered across its open prairies and deciduous forests, and that's not counting the lakes that are shared across the Canadian border or with other states.

When thinking of Minnesota, most probably think of the Twin Cities (the massive Minneapolis-Saint Paul that is home to three-fifths of the population). Far fewer think of the vast woodlands that make it heaven for outdoorsmen and women.

Every September, one of the most popular recreational outdoor activities in Minnesota is waterfowl hunting for ducks and geese. Since there is no shortage of lakes in Minnesota, there is also no shortage of locations to go waterfowl hunting.

While many Minnesotans hunt ducks and geese from ashore near bodies of water, many others embark on boats to take shots at the elusive birds from the middle of the lakes. And while waterfowl hunting from a boat is certainly a major thrill…, it also brings with it a significant risk.

The state of Minnesota mandates that waterfowlers have life jackets in their vessels at all times, with at least one jacket per passenger. Unfortunately, these legal requirements only go so far in actually ensuring safety. Many hunters will bring life jackets into their boats, but not actually wear them while hunting.

And while life jackets can be very bulky and cumbersome to have on your person, which can disrupt the process of bringing your shotgun to your shoulder to take a shot at the birds, they can still work wonders to save your life should you fall into the frigid waters.

Even if you're confident in your swimming abilities, the weight of your shotgun and other hunting equipment can weigh you down and make your survival efforts more difficult. That's also not to mention that in the fall and winter months especially, the lakes of Minnesota can become exceptionally frigid and result in hypothermia very fast should you fall in. The winters of Minnesota are already known for being exceptionally long and brutal, meaning they can already set in during the fall hunting months when waterfowlers are out on the lakes.

The possibility of falling into an ice-cold lake is one of the biggest risks that waterfowl hunters who hunt from boats face.

This is precisely what one hunter named Dan found out in the fall of 1984.

* * *

In September of 1984, three Minnesotan hunting buddies by the names of John, Erik, and Dan went out duck hunting on Lake Puposky. Accompanying them was John's Brittany Spaniel dog, Brandy.

Lake Puposky has long been popular with waterfowl hunters and is located in Northern Minnesota. The lake consists of a large island and a smaller island within its waters, both of which are frequented by duck hunters. Like most other lakes in Minnesota, the lake gets very cold during the fall and winter months.

When the three arrived at the lake early in the morning, it was as chilly of a day as any other. Loading up into John's duck boat, which measured around 12 feet in length, the three hunters set out on the east side of the lake towards the big island in the middle. There were other duck hunters present on the south side of the big island as well.

Unfortunately, the trio would soon make a few misguided decisions that they would pay the price for soon. Most notably, they made perhaps the biggest duck hunter boating mistake: while they had enough life jackets in the boat to satisfy Minnesota's legal requirements, they weren't wearing them.

The three unloaded on the east side of the island to look for ducks, with Brandy still tied in the boat so she wouldn't run along the beach.

They spotted a duck that took off from the island and flew about two hundred yards away before descending back into the water. Unable to get a shot off from the island, Dan opted to take off after the duck in the boat with his shotgun. John and Erik remained back on the island.

Dan departed from the island in the boat, but the vessel was not balancing well in the water with him in the back. He also wasn't wearing a life jacket. Brandy was still tied to the inside of the boat as well.

While Dan was searching for the duck in the boat, with John and Erik still on shore, the boat suddenly flipped over into the water.

On instinct, Dan reached over to grab Brandy as they both plunged into the freezing water, and all of the life jackets blew away in the wind before settling in the water out of Dan's reach.

Further complicating matters was the fact that the vessel was an older hunting boat that lacked level flotation. The boat was hardly afloat after it had tipped over, with only the upside-down front tip above water level. The motor of the boat was weighing down the back end deep into the water.

Dan tried to stabilize himself over the boat, only for it to sink further under the water. Meanwhile, he was also trying to grab Brandy who was trapped and thrashing under the boat.

Meanwhile, John and Erik witnessed what was happening from the shoreline. Erik froze up, while John immediately started running down to the south side of the island to warn the other hunters around half a mile away.

But his heart soon sank as he saw the other hunters were in their own motorboat heading away. Firing multiple rounds from his shotgun into the air didn't gain their attention.

Frantically, he spun back around and ran back up to the north side of the island, about a full mile long. Along the way, he passed by Erik, who was sitting on a bench and sobbing uncontrollably.

Realizing that no other hunters were present on the island, John knew he had to take matters into his own hands to save Dan. Peering across the narrows on the north end of the island, he saw a farmhouse on the mainland.

John dived into the water and started swimming across the lake with his hunting clothes still on, but he couldn't make it because the clothes and equipment on him were too heavy. He quickly returned to shore, disrobed down to his underwear, and then tried again.

He was already shivering horribly from the freezing water at this point and knew that hypothermia was likely to set in if he tried again, but John also knew that his friend Dan was in a far worse condition back in the boat.

John dove back into the lake and trod water all the way to the shoreline of the mainland. With any luck, he thought, he'd make it to the mainland and the farmhouse before hypothermia set in. And with any more luck after that, he'd find a boat or get help to go back and rescue Dan...

* * *

Dan was desperately treading water. He was shivering violently from the freezing water, and his hefty hunting clothes were making it difficult for him to stay afloat.

Brandy had gone still and silent, having tragically drowned in the water under the boat. Dan was on his own.

To reduce the weight on the boat, Dan decided to remove the motor off of the end of the transom, or the stern of the boat. To accomplish this, he needed to dive under to get the latches on the motor unscrewed. Still shivering violently as hypothermia set in, Dan finally managed to get the motor loose after multiple attempts.

The motor loosened free from the transom and sank into the lake as the boat finally started to move up more toward the surface...but then the safety chain of the motor caught onto the boat.

With the motor sinking fast, it dragged the boat fourteen inches deeper under the water with it, worsening the situation further.

Dan now knew that the situation was hopeless. He couldn't swim back to shore, he couldn't float over the boat, and hypothermia was setting in hard. The blood left Dan's extremities and the inner warmth began to deplete from his core. He was already shaking and shivering violently and now it became even worse, to the point that he couldn't even think as he lost focus.

Just as Dan was about to accept his apparent fate, he thought about how his parents would take the loss of a son, and he prayed for more time. With what little mental strength he had left, he prayed that he would be a good person to his friends and family for the rest of his life if only he could have more time.

Just then, the boat popped back up to the surface. The motor's safety chain had somehow slipped from the boat, permitting it to levitate back to the surface of the water.

Then the faint sounds of a boat motor steadily getting louder and louder reached Dan's ears. He looked over at the sound and saw another boat with John, albeit very wet and in his underwear, coming toward him.

Just as Dan realized that his desperate prayers had been answered, he blacked out.

* * *

When Dan came to and regained consciousness, he was wrapped in a blanket and placed in front of a warm oven.

John and Erik were with him, and John explained what had happened. He'd made it across the narrows on the north end of the lake, ran up to the farm, and found the boat with a trailer in the barn.

He'd plugged the boat's drain hole with a rag and then pulled the trailer to the shoreline with his brute strength. Launching the boat, he'd got the motor started and immediately set out to Dan's position, rescuing him just in the nick of time.

The older couple who owned the farm returned around the time as John was finishing the story. Though shocked by what they saw, they assisted the hunters with getting Dan back to town to start his recovery.

* * *

The biggest lesson from this harrowing true survival story is to have a never quit attitude when you find yourself in a survival situation. Both Dan and John refused to quit no matter the odds. Despite being plunged into the frigid waters, Dan stayed calm and did everything he could to get the boat afloat so he wouldn't drown, and he held on until help came. Had the boat not stayed fully afloat, Dan would have expended more energy trying to swim and likely would have drowned.

John never stopped until he found a solution to find his friend. He ran all over the island to search for help, and when there was none, he swam across the freezing waters to find help. And when he still couldn't find help then, he took matters into his own hands, located the boat, and dragged it all the way back to the shoreline before setting out to rescue Dan.

Just think - John could have stopped when he didn't find help on the island when he needed to swim across the narrows to the shoreline, or when he needed to drag the extra boat back to the shoreline. Any one of these would have stopped an individual who had lesser inner fortitude, but it didn't stop John because he was bound and determined to do everything possible to rescue his friend.

This stood in contrast to Erik, who did exactly what you shouldn't do in a life-or-death survival situation and froze up and broke down sobbing on the shoreline while John was out finding and dragging the extra boat back.

Neither John nor Dan gave up; John never gave up on rescuing his friend and Dan never gave up on staying alive. And that was the driving force that ensured Dan made it out alive.

CHAPTER THREE

THREE DAYS ALONE

An Oregon hunter found out that just because you often frequent the same hunting area doesn't mean you can't get lost. And when you do get lost, you'll have to be prepared and act quickly and decisively if you want to make it out alive.

What would you do if you embarked on a hunting trip only to lose your way and find yourself alone in the woods?

That's exactly the question that confronted 34-year-old Oregonian native Nicholas Benim in October 2017.

Nicholas was always what most people would consider a living example of the avid outdoorsman. Having spent a lot of time in the mountains and forests of western Oregon where he learned to fish, hunt, and hike, he was also intimately familiar with the area.

Once a year, Nicholas always embarked with a buddy on a camping and hunting trip deep into the forests by Hideaway Lake, in the general proximity of Mount Hood. The highest mountain in Oregon and the fourth highest in the Cascade Range, Mount Hood attracts millions of adventurers every year, including climbers, skiers, hikers, campers, and fishermen.

The Mount Hood National Forest area also attracts plenty of hunters who come for elk and deer in the fall months. Several of these hunters, such as Nicholas, come to hunt the forests near Mount Hood every year.

But as Nicholas soon found out, just because you frequent a hunting area and are familiar with it doesn't mean that you'll be safe. Accidents can still happen, and you can still get lost.

* * *

Every year during hunting season, Nicholas traveled to Hideaway Lake with a group of hunting buddies for a camping and hunting trip. 2017 was no exception.

On Sunday afternoon, Nicholas and his hunting partner headed out together into the woods with the rest of their group to go after deer. After a few hours, deep in the maze of ponderosa pines, Nicholas realized that he had walked too far ahead of his partner.

At first, he wasn't worried. His hunting buddy couldn't be far, he figured, so Nicholas turned around and followed the trail back to go find him.

Then, it slowly dawned upon Nicholas that his surroundings were not right. He had followed the wrong trail back.

Attempting to regain control over his bearings, Nicholas walked back the way he had come in an attempt to locate the original trail he had come down, but he couldn't find it.

Coming by the side of a steep slope, Nicholas attempted to walk carefully to the other side, with his backpack and rifle weighing down over his shoulders.

Suddenly, he lost his balance and his boot slipped. Nicholas crashed down the side of the slope all the way to the bottom.

Quickly assessing his injuries, Nicholas realized that thankfully, other than a few scrapes and bruises, he had suffered no injuries. But he also realized that he was lost. He had been unable to locate the trail at the top of the hillside from which he had just come crashing down, and he didn't know where he was at the bottom of the hill either.

It was just starting to register in Nicholas's mind that he was now experiencing what every hunter dreaded: he was officially lost in the middle of the forest!

It was late afternoon by this point, and the air was beginning to chill as dusk would be setting in soon. Rather than attempt to walk out that night, Nicholas decided that he would bunk down and wait for morning.

The good news for Nicholas was that despite being lost, he'd come prepared. His years of hunting, camping, and backpacking in Oregon's mountains had taught him the critical lesson to never go walking alone into the woods without survival equipment. Every time Nicholas went out hunting, he always brought a pack of survival items with him, and this trip was no exception. It very well may have been the decision that saved his life.

That night, Nicholas was able to build a fire using fire starters he had in his pack. He also had a solar survival blanket in his pack that he used to wrap around himself. He didn't get much sleep that night because he had to repeatedly tend to the fire and add more wood to keep it going, but this was necessary to stay warm - which was most critical to his survival.

Had Nicholas been unable to get a fire going or had he lacked the survival blanket it would have been a very cold and potentially life-threatening night?

The next morning was Monday, and despite being tired, Nicholas was determined to find his way out. Moving his way through the woods, he eventually came to a clearing. Here he stopped, hoping that someone would find him. With any luck, he would run into other hunters in the area, or his friend would have sent out notifications to emergency rescue teams that he was missing. If a search and rescue helicopter were to circle overhead, it would have the best chance of finding him in a clearing like this one, he thought.

Nicholas spent the rest of the day in this clearing. He located some fallen logs and opted to sleep under them for the night for shelter.

Yet again, Nicholas' prior preparation came to his aid. He had a little food and water in his pack that he used for sustenance, and he also had spare clothes that he wrapped around himself for extra warmth along with his blanket, and he used his backpack as a pillow.

Nicholas slept and wished for better luck in the morning.

* * *

While Nicholas had accurately predicted that searchers were out looking for him, what he had failed to predict was that they were searching in the completely wrong area.

That was because he had wandered very far from his original location. His friend had informed the search and rescue teams of where and when he had disappeared, but this was a significant distance from the clearing in which Nicholas now waited.

When Nicholas awoke the next day, there was still no help and he had run out of water. He was also beginning to feel the negative effects of dehydration. Searching the area around the clearing, he came to a running stream.

Nicholas knew he needed the water, but unfortunately, he had neglected to pack water purification tablets or a filtration device with him.

Every single cell in the human body requires water to function, and Nicholas also knew that he needed water to keep up his stamina and mental functions to get out alive. So, he took a risk and drank the water out of the stream directly.

Nicholas continued to walk on through the woods with his pack and rifle slung across his back. Coming to another stream, he attempted to cross it by stepping over rocks and logs jutting out of the water, but the heavy pack and rifle over his back made it difficult for him to keep his balance.

Suddenly, he lost his footing and plunged directly into the icy water. Getting out of the water as quickly as possible, Nicholas removed his clothing and got another fire going with his fire starters. He spent the rest of the day drying out his clothes by the fire and spent another nearly sleepless night in the woods.

The next day, Nicholas' clothes were not completely dry, but they were significantly drier than when he had fallen into the stream, so he could wear them again and stay on the move. And most importantly, he was still alive and determined to make it out.

Despite being wet and cold, Nicholas managed to walk eight miles through the woods. He eventually found a few deer, ironically the same game that he had come to the woods to hunt for. But Nicholas was no longer in any mood for a hunt, despite still having his rifle with him.

He followed the game trail the deer were using, and the trail eventually led him to a paved road. Nicholas walked along the road until he saw a forest service truck cruising toward him.

Nicholas waved the truck down, and the forest service employee, Mike Burri, immediately pulled over at the sight of the wet and ragged man who had just emerged out of the woods.

Nicholas was alive and rescued.

* * *

There are two critical lessons that we can learn from Nicholas's ordeal. The first is to always come prepared. Nicholas had a backpack with him, in which he had critical survival tools including fire-starting devices, food and water, a survival blanket, and extra clothing. Each of these items assisted Nicholas greatly during his experience in the freezing Oregon woods, and collectively they may have saved his life.

Granted, Nicholas didn't have every survival item with him he should have had. He didn't have a water filter or purification tablets with him, for instance, and he took a significant risk by drinking out of the water stream directly.

Drinking untreated water leaves a huge chance of ingesting dangerous bacteria. In retrospect, Nicholas acknowledged the big risk he took by drinking the water directly from the source, but he also claimed that drinking the water and getting hydrated kept him alive and helped him walk out.

Overall, Nicholas was much more prepared than many people who ventured out into the woods. Just a handful of simple survival items such as a solar blanket and fire-starting devices can be the difference between life and death.

The second lesson is to take action quickly. The moment Nicholas fell into the freezing stream, for example, he didn't waste any time. He immediately got out of the water, stripped off his clothes, and got a fire going to warm and dry off his clothing. Had he wasted any more time, hypothermia could have set in, to the point that he couldn't get a fire going, in which case he almost certainly would have died.

Preparation for the worst, and quick thinking when things did turn for the worst, are what ensured Nicholas made it out alive from his ordeal by Mount Hood.

Nicholas's feet remained very swollen for several days after his misadventure, but other than that and a few scrapes and blisters, he was in remarkably good condition. The Sheriff's Office of Clackamas County had been alerted of his disappearance the morning following his disappearance. His hunting group had expected him to return that night, but when he never did, they went to the sheriff's office to alert them about his disappearance.

As if his survival wasn't remarkable enough, Nicholas was also in excellent spirits after the incident.

Burri, the forest service employee who rescued Nicholas recalled him casually saying, "hey, I've been lost for four days, can you take me into town?" As he pulled up to him on the side of the road.

What's also remarkable is the sheer amount of territory that Nicholas covered. Burri estimated that Nicholas had walked more than twenty-five miles. That was why the search and rescue teams deployed to find him had such a challenging time. Nicholas was a fast walker despite walking over the wilderness ground without trails.

Today, Nicholas is still alive and well and he's enjoying life with his wife and five children.

"Nick was prepared," his father Bobby said after the event. "He had a compass, he had a lighter, a water bottle, a little bit of food, he had a solar blanket. He was able to make fires at night."

Wherever and whenever you go hunting or hiking out in the woods, always go prepared with survival items. Nicholas was a frequent hunter of the area he was in, but even that didn't stop him from getting lost out there. It's a crystal-clear reminder that you must always be prepared no matter what.

CHAPTER FOUR

FALLING DOWN

Tree stands are popular with deer hunters for their ability to help them ambush their prey from close range. But a Georgia hunter found out the hard way that a tree stand can just as easily become a hunter's worst nightmare.

Two activities that Dwight Jones enjoyed more than any other were - hunting deer and flying airplanes. He was fortunate enough to have spent nearly four decades of his life doing both.

As someone who piloted airplanes for a career and regularly hunted in Georgia's backwoods as a hobby, Dwight was ingrained with a survivalist mindset. Pilots are tasked with the responsibility of protecting the lives of dozens if not hundreds of passengers on board their plane, and Dwight was reminded of that every time he sat in the front seat in the cockpit. His number one priority every time was to protect the lives of everyone on board that plane.

In other words, Dwight was always primarily concerned with protecting the lives of other people. It wasn't until a hunting trip that he would be confronted with needing to protect his own.

"It has always struck me that the parallels that exist between the aviation industry and the hunting industry are very similar," Dwight recalled, "what we do can be dangerous or even fatal; however, if done responsibly and with adequate care, both can be very safe."

It was the fall of 2017, and Dwight was doing what he loved most when he wasn't flying airplanes: hunting deer in the lush woods of Georgia.

Like many hunters in Georgia (and throughout the world, for that matter), Dwight liked to hunt deer using tree stands. Tree stands are elevated platforms designed to be attached to a tree. They allow a hunter to sit and watch for deer anywhere from 10 to 20 feet above the ground.

Deer tree stands can provide hunters with numerous advantages. Not only do they offer the hunter a superior view from which they can look for wild game, but they also allow the hunter to remain hidden by staying out of the line of sight of a deer. Deer has an acute sense of smell, but the fact that the hunters are elevated so far up above the ground also helps to hide their scent as well.

Another advantage of tree stands is that they allow the hunter to get much closer to the deer than they otherwise could. That's because since the deer won't see or smell the hunter (at least in theory), they'll walk close to the stand, allowing the hunter to get a close and clear shot.

In other words, deer stands help to hide and better facilitate ambushing deer rather than actively hunting them. Deer hunters will often follow a strategy of scouting areas that are rich in deer signs (such as droppings or tracks) before the hunt and then set up their tree stands in the optimal location.

They'll then arrive at the site early in the morning when it is still dark outside and climb a ladder up to the stand. Then, the hunter sits and waits for a deer to come trotting down the game trail sometime after it's gotten light outside.

This was a strategy that had proven successful for Dwight in many prior hunts throughout his 40 years of hunting, so there was no reason not to try it again. Dwight was also acutely aware of the risks of using a tree stand: most notably, the possibility of accidentally falling out of the stand and falling hard to the ground.

That's why Dwight always installed a safety line to each hunting stand he had set up…or, at least, almost every stand. A safety line is secured to the tree and then also secured to the hunter. Should the hunter fall out of the stand, the line will then hold them and prevent them from falling to the ground. This one stand that was involved in Dwight's accident, however, was the only one to which he opted not to attach a safety line.

It is critical to install a safety line for any tree stand. Even a stand that's only elevated five to six feet above the ground can prove fatal to a hunter if they fall out. All it takes is for the hunter to fall and hit their head at the right angle, and severe internal damage within the skull or other parts of the body can either kill them instantly or leave life-altering consequences if they do survive.

That being said, hunters in Georgia are no strangers to risks. Venomous snakes are a major threat in southern states like Georgia, and hunters have to take every available precaution to both avoid them and protect themselves in the event they encounter one.

That's why hunters in the American Deep South often wear what are called 'snake boots,' or boots that go almost up to the knee and are constructed out of durable puncture-proof materials that can resist snake bites. Most snake boots for hunters are made out of rubber, leather, or polyurethane. All also come with snake-guard lining that further makes them impenetrable to the fangs of a snake.

As Dwight would soon come to realize, his snake boots would provide him with additional protection beyond shielding his legs against snake bites.

Dwight headed out into the woods of Georgia on a normal October day. He went to his tree stand, wearing his snake boots. It was a typical hunting morning.

Tree stands are designed to lock securely onto trees to hold the weight of the occupants inside. They also come with ladders or climbing steps to assist the hunter in ascending them.

While some deer hunters will attach and take down their tree stands with each hunting year, other hunters will leave the stand secured to the tree for many years. This saves them the hassle of needing to come out each year to reattach the stand.

Dwight came to the same tree stand he left in place every year to wait for a deer to come down the game trail.

But Dwight made one critical mistake. He had forgotten to return to the tree stand before the hunt to check that it was still secured to the tree. Even though modern-day deer hunting tree stands are durable and can attach very snugly to trees, they still require routine maintenance and should be checked consistently to make sure they're still working.

As Dwight would admit after the incident, he had neglected to check his tree stand before the hunt, and it would cost him.

Arriving just as the first light of dawn was starting to break out over the trees, Dwight looked up to see that his usual tree stand was where he had left it. It was exactly twenty-two feet up the tree.

He started to ascend the climbing steps to the platform, making it to the very last step just before the main platform when suddenly something gave way, and he plummeted back toward the ground!

As Dwight fell back, his body rotated vertically so that his head was now pointed down toward the ground and both his feet were now aimed up at the sky.

Even though it was only a couple of seconds before Dwight hit the ground, it was enough time for his mind to process that if he landed on his head hard enough, it would be very bad for him…if not death, then surely, he would suffer paralysis or some sort of a lifelong physical disability. Dwight also thought that he would lose consciousness the moment he hit the ground.

Sure enough, Dwight hit the ground hard…, but instead of losing consciousness, his entire upper body erupted in what felt like a crescendo of fire overtaking his upper body. The feeling was unlike anything he had ever before experienced, but strangely enough, as Dwight later reported, it wasn't one of pain.

After a moment to get a hold of his bearings and realize that he wasn't dead or unconscious, Dwight immediately began to assess his situation.

Dwight's first thought, once he realized that he had miraculously avoided serious injury, was one of anger at his negligence in checking the tree stand to confirm it was still sturdy.

Then he realized that his head and neck were not in contact with the ground...rather, they were in contact with his backpack, which was filled with survival and hunting items. This pack had broken his fall and prevented his head from hitting the hard ground; if not for this, it's highly likely that Dwight would have broken his neck and experienced life-altering injuries.

But that wasn't the only reason Dwight had avoided death or horrific physical wounds. His left snake boot had caught onto one of the steps, to the point that the boot was punctured through and ripped open. This action had caused Dwight's body to rotate from 90 degrees to 70 degrees, changing the angle at which his head hit the backpack on the ground. This alone may have saved his life as well.

Dwight remained still on the ground where he had fallen for several minutes. As he was comprehending that he was alive and still conscious, he began to wiggle his toes and fingers. That was a good sign. He also moved his head around to see if any bones were jutting out anywhere or if any limbs were misaligned, and to his relief, he could see no signs of fractures or open wounds at all.

His neck was very sore, and it made moving his head around difficult. But he didn't have a headache, which told Dwight that he most likely did not have a concussion. Another miracle.

Dwight's feelings of shock and anger at himself for failing to check the tree stand before climbing it began to turn to feelings of joy and elatedness, as he realized that not only was he alive but that he was almost entirely unharmed other than for a sore neck. Dwight thanked God for his survival and also vowed at this moment that if he indeed survived and made it out alive, he would inform other hunters he knew to be more careful regarding hunting stands and the possibility of falls.

With full control of his body, despite the soreness of his neck, Dwight managed to dig his phone out of his pocket. He called a hunting friend who was also an early riser and let him know what had happened and his location, in case he couldn't walk out. He then called another friend who was a doctor; the doctor advised him to go to an ER immediately.

Dwight slowly picked himself up from the ground. Though still a little dazed, he continued to experience full control over his movements and body. It was incredible. He made his way back to his vehicle through the woods; he remembered exactly where he had parked and how to get there, so his mind was still working properly as well.

He then drove over to the ER in Macon for an assessment. The medical staff was alarmed to hear that he had fallen twenty-two feet but amazed to see that he was fully alive and functioning well.

The medical staff informed Dwight that falling down over a hard surface from above 20 feet greatly maximizes the chance and extent of physical injury versus falling from less than 20 feet. That's why medical staff are trained to be prepared for the potential of more trauma for injured patients who fell more than twenty feet. Dwight then realized just how lucky he was.

The staff carefully assessed Dwight for any broken bones or internal injuries, but they couldn't find any. It was very, very rare that a patient who had fallen more than twenty feet came to them in as good of condition as Dwight had.

More doctor friends came into Dwight's room and assessed him as well. They were all likewise amazed that he had survived the fall without a single bone fracture or internal injury. It was as if Dwight had never fallen at all!

One reason why Dwight came out of the accident in such great shape, his doctors informed him, is because he was in incredibly decent shape for a man who was 50 years old. Dwight was always careful to watch his weight and to do basic strength and cardio training. Had he been fifty pounds heavier or had softer muscles, the outcome would almost certainly have been much worse.

* * *

Dwight Jones got extremely lucky. Or as he would say later upon reflection, what happened was truly a "pure miracle."

Dwight never let his guard down when it came to public safety with flying airplanes. But he did get his guard down regarding his own safety, and what happened to him was a fierce reminder that he could never let his guard down like that again.

After the incident, Dwight took the time to study what had happened and think about what had gone wrong.

Dwight uses multiple stands each year, but this one stand he used on that fateful morning was the one he had forgotten to check or to attach a lifeline to. Had he installed the lifeline to the tree, it would have prevented him from falling to the ground.

Tree stand lifelines are very affordable and rarely cost more than twenty dollars, so there's no excuse not to install one on your tree stand. That's why Dwight now makes it a habit to ensure that every tree stand that he uses must have a safety line.

Dwight also inspected the tree stand itself. As a hunter who regularly uses tree stands, Dwight estimated that he set up and took down over fifty lock-on tree stands a year. He did it so often, in fact, that he estimated he could set up or take down a lock-on tree stand with his eyes closed.

So, if Dwight was so proficient at setting up tree stands, how was it that this one tree stand that caused the accident was the one he didn't check before attempting to climb it?

It was the same reason this was the same tree stand he didn't attach a safety line to - simple negligence.

Dwight only ever used high-quality lock-ons, that are strong and durable. The lock-on he used for this particular tree stand was no different, but it was a different type of lock-on than he normally used.

The normal lock-ons that Dwight used had a chain receiver attached to the lock-on itself. But the lock-on device that Dwight used for this tree stand used a ratchet-type receiver instead. The ratchets for these kinds of lock-on devices need to be sporadically opened up further to account for tree growth.

As a result, the ratchet was spread incredibly thin, as the tree had grown in the months since Dwight had installed the stand. So, when he started ascending the climbing steps, the weight was too great for the already-stretched ratchet, and it gave way by the time he neared the top.

After the incident, Dwight said that he was aware of this issue with ratchet-style lock-ons, but that he had neglected to check the ratchet before he used the tree stand. The ratchet was also located on the opposite side of the tree from where the stand was positioned, and Dwight approached the tree stand from the front. Since the ratchet was out of view, it didn't cross his mind to check the ratchet before he ascended.

Had Dwight simply remembered to check the ratchet to account for the growth of the tree, the entire incident could have been avoided.

The good news is that inspecting the stand after the incident showed Dwight yet another reason he was so fortunate. Even though the stand had given way under his weight due to the stretched top ratchet strap, the bottom safety strap had held on. This stopped the entire stand from falling from the tree - had it done so, it could have crashed over Dwight on the ground and caused severe injury.

The good news is that Dwight realized his error and informed his hunting friends of what happened so they would avoid the same mistake. He also recounted his story to hunting magazines and newspapers to help spread the word about what happened.

* * *

Tree stands are in very widespread use by hunters all over the world. What happened to Dwight could happen to any deer hunter who uses a tree stand.

Dwight fell twenty-two feet upside down, but a couple of coincidences saved his life. The first was his head landing on his backpack rather than the ground itself. And the second was his snake boot catching onto his stand, changing the angle of his fall.

A third major help for Dwight was the fact that he was in good physical shape and always kept a close eye on his weight and strength. This likely saved him from suffering life-altering injuries.

Dwight did many things right after the incident as well that should serve as a valuable lesson to us. Rather than brushing off the incident, Dwight put in the effort to learn about what went wrong to avoid making the same mistake again. He then put his story out there so other deer hunters could be prevented from making the same mistake as well.

To this day, Dwight still keeps a positive attitude after his experience. "We are all blessed to have family, friends and the outdoors," he says. "Please be safe and enjoy a great deer season!"

CHAPTER FIVE

ONE WEEK IN GRIZZLY COUNTRY

When two grizzly bear hunters ventured out into one of the most inhospitable and remote regions in Alaska, everything that could go wrong went wrong. Only one of them made it out alive.

There is no place on Earth like Alaska. Truly a land of unspoiled beauty, Alaska is home to majestic snow-capped mountains, sprawling green forests, vast tundra, damp wetlands, steep hillsides, and never-ending rivers. The land is also home to an abundance of wildlife, including moose, Dall sheep, caribou, wolves, and the big prize among North American hunters, the grizzly bear.

The Alaskan wilderness is also among the most remote, brutal, and inhospitable regions on the planet. It's a major risk for anyone who goes there to hunt or hike out in the woods because, if you find yourself stranded out there, it will be very difficult for search and rescue teams to find you due to the vast expanse of land to cover. And if they do find you, the elements very well may kill you first.

Even in the summer months in Alaska when the days are warmer and brighter, at nighttime the temperatures can easily and quickly drop to below freezing. It's also common for it to rain in Alaska for several days straight, and this combined with the freezing temperatures alone is what can make survival so difficult.

Nonetheless, thousands of hunters brave Alaska's beautiful and brutal wilderness every year just for a chance to take a shot at a moose or a bear. Some of these hunters live in Alaska and are very used to the unforgiving terrain of the state. But many other hunters travel the long journey to the state for a hunt instead.

Adrian Knopps was one of these hunters.

A lifelong hunter who always dreamed of hunting for grizzly bears in Alaska, Adrian was an electrician who was native to Michigan. He was more familiar with the flat woodlands of the American Midwest than the towering mountains of Alaska. But he was an experienced hunter and an outdoorsman nonetheless, and he felt he was ready for his lifelong dream of a hunting trip north to Alaska.

Little did Adrian know that he would soon find himself in the fiercest struggle for his life, braving bitter temperatures, never-ending rainstorms, the threat of bears and wolves, and 70-mile-per-hour winds to make it out alive.

* * *

Adrian was 51 years old, and he had plenty of years of hunting under his belt. The idea of hunting for bears in Alaska had always fascinated him, not only to experience the sheer majesty of Alaska's wild landscape but also because Alaska is one of the absolute best places in the world to go hunting for brown bears.

Arriving in mid-September 2013, Adrian met up with Garrett Hagen, a 24-year-old Alaskan native who would serve as his hunting partner.

The plan was simple: Adrian and Garrett would meet in the town of Ketchikan in Southeastern Alaska. They would then embark together on a 10-day hunt for grizzly bears deep in the Alaskan wilderness. To access the wilderness area that they would hunt, they would travel in Garrett's 50-foot boat up the Chickamin River. They would then anchor the boat off the mouth of a river when they had traveled up deep enough, and then travel further up the narrower areas of the river in a seven-foot-long skiff, or small coastal boat, to one of the islands known to be home to lots of bears.

The area they were headed into was known for teeming with bears specifically, and Adrian was extremely excited at the prospect of fulfilling his dream of successfully hunting a grizzly bear in the woods of Alaska.

At first, everything went according to plan.

The two traveled in the larger boat and then anchored it in a harbor at the mouth of the Chickamin River. They then transferred to the skiff and headed upriver for about five miles. On that day it was cool at around 60 degrees Fahrenheit, the sun was out, and the skies were clear. It was the perfect weather for a bear hunt.

Adrian and Garrett spent three days camping out on the island in the Alaskan wilderness while searching for bears. On the third day of the trip, Adrian's lifelong dream came true. The pair spotted a brown bear, Adrian took the rifle to his shoulder, aimed carefully, and fired a single shot.

The bear was down, and Adrian's dream was fulfilled.

The two spent several hours skinning and butchering the animal. They were located about a half mile away from the skiff.

The bear had several hundred pounds of meat, none of which Adrian wanted to waste. But their skiff was far too small to hold the weight of him, Garrett, and all of the bear meat at the same time. So, the pair developed a plan: together, they would haul the bear meat down to the coast and load up as much as they could into the skiff. Then Garrett would board the skiff and transport the meat back to their main boat about five miles down the river.

Adrian would then wait in that location, and when Garrett returned later, they would load up the rest of the meat and set out back to the boat together.

Everything had gone according to plan so far, so the two had no reason to think that wouldn't continue.

Garrett estimated that it would take between two and three hours for him to return to the original boat, unload the meat, and then go back to pick up Adrian and the rest of the meat.

With the skiff fully loaded with bear meat, Garrett boarded and took off while Adrian stayed behind. Adrian stood watching on the shoreline. It would be the last time Adrian ever saw Garrett.

* * *

When Garrett didn't return after the two or three hours he had estimated, Adrian wasn't too concerned. Garrett must have just been taking his time or underestimated how long it would take him to unload everything.

But when daytime turned to dusk, Adrian began to get a little apprehensive. And when dusk turned to night with still no sign of Garrett, it slowly dawned upon Adrian that he would be staying for the rest of the night.

Adrian had no vessel of his own so he couldn't travel down the river himself. The water was also much too freezing to even consider the possibility of swimming. He was also out of cell and internet service, so there was no chance of contacting Garrett or anybody else for that matter.

Still, Adrian tried to stay optimistic. Even if he had to spend the night alone in the Alaskan wilderness, he could do it. He had spent plenty of nights out alone in the Michigan woods before.

But there was a problem. Adrian and Garrett had only brought three days' worth of supplies in the skiff. Even though they had planned and prepared to be out in the wilderness for 10 days, the rest of the food and supplies were back on the main boat. The idea was they could travel back to the main boat in the skiff to resupply when they needed. Now Adrian was alone in the woods with very little in the way of sustenance and supplies.

Adrian took inventory of what little food and water he had. His water canteen was only partially full, and he had a grand total of four granola bars. Hopefully, that would last him until Garrett returned, he thought.

The next morning came. Adrian had gotten truly little sleep the night before, partially because of the stress and also because the temperatures had fallen to near freezing over the night.

The entire next day, Adrian waited, but Garrett still never returned.

Something had happened, Adrian knew. And now that he was officially stranded on this island in the Alaskan wild, he also knew that he had no chance of walking out. He had to stay put, last as long as he could, and hope that help would come to him.

Adrian identified wolf and bear tracks on the ground and moved his position away from them. He selected the highest point that he could find on the tidal flats and decided to take what little shelter he could underneath a driftwood tree by a mound.

He gathered wood to make a fire and managed to get one going. But it rained by the second day, putting out the flames, and the water from the river began to rise and carried his wood away.

Despite the adverse conditions and the threat of the rising water, Adrian decided to stick near the river instead of up on the hill because of the bear and wolf tracks that he had spotted there. The roots of the fallen tree were over fifteen feet in the area, and he clung onto them when the water rose from the river. He dared not venture up to the drier ground up on the hill.

All this time, Adrian knew that something was wrong with Garrett, but he didn't know what had happened. His mind was racing between what had happened to his hunting partner, if help would come his way, and how he would stay alive until help did arrive.

It didn't take long for Adrian's water supply to run out. When it did, he resorted to drinking rainwater that gathered on rocks, leaves, and trees. Drinking rainwater was safer than drinking water out of the river or any streams.

Getting any sleep was also immensely difficult for Adrian. The island was the subject of repeated rain, making the ground very wet and soggy. Laying down on the ground would soak him through, and in the kind of freezing temperatures that night brought, hypothermia would become a very real possibility. To get around this, Adrian laid pine boughs down on the ground and placed his back against a tree. It wasn't as comfortable, but it kept him drier than laying on the ground.

Adrian began to think that the worst had happened to Garrett. There was no way that Garrett could have reached the boat and forgotten his way back. This sunk Adrian's heart further, not only for the loss of his friend but because it also meant that Garrett could not have alerted the authorities to Adrian's location.

The only person who could alert rescue teams, Adrian thought, was his wife back home in Michigan. He was supposed to call her after seven days, and if he didn't, he believed she would call the proper authorities to send search and rescue teams out after him. This was the only sliver of hope that Adrian had for his rescue. It was this hope that helped him, mentally and physically, to endure the extreme weather conditions for the duration of that week.

On the fifth day of Adrian's survival, a massive wind and rainstorm hit the island. The winds reached insane speeds of 70 miles per hour and thrashed the trees around violently. Adrian was forced to hug the ground to avoid getting blown around by the rain, and the rain poured and poured all night.

Adrian became soaked to the bone, and he spent the rest of the night huddled up and shivering violently. When the winds became too great to hold out against on his own, he used a paracord to lash himself down to tree roots that were jutting out of the ground. Somehow, he was able to live through the night. It wasn't until after daybreak that the winds and rain began to ease up.

It was on the sixth day that Adrian began to believe help would never come his way. Even if search and rescue teams were looking for him, they may have thought he was in a different area and were searching in the completely wrong places.

Accepting his fate, Adrian scratched a goodbye note to his wife and loved ones in the stock of his hunting rifle.

He wrote:

> *'A Knopps stuck on river tidal flat for 5 days. Cold wet no food. Garrett Hagen, Craig, AK died taking a big bear to boat 9-15-13.'*

On the sixth night, Adrian lay down next to the rifle and figured it would be his last night alive.

When he awoke on the seventh day, Adrian was completely depleted of energy. He couldn't even stand, and even if he could, where could he go? Slowly, he waited for the inevitable and to die on this random island in the Alaskan wilderness.

"Please God," Adrian prayed under his breath that help would somehow find his way.

Adrian figured his prayer was his final Hail Mary. He was all out of options, out of food, out of any drinkable water, out of strength, and nearing the end of his willpower to stay alive. This was it.

Adrian closed his eyes and waited for death to overtake him. Two hours had passed before he heard a low buzzing in the distance. Initially, he thought it was nothing, but ever so slowly, the buzzing became louder and louder.

Soon, Adrian was able to recognize the buzzing as a helicopter. A wave of hope swept into Adrian's heart. If he was going to be discovered, it was now. His prayers had been answered!

"It was the most wonderful sound I had heard," Adrian recounted of the moment he recognized the buzzing as that of a helicopter.

With what little strength he had, Adrian dragged himself from the dense forest over to the open shoreline by the water. He waved his colored life vest out in the open, and it didn't take long for the helicopter to spot him.

As the helicopter lowered itself by Adrian's position, he recognized it as a US Coast Guard helicopter. Coast Guard servicemen disembarked and ran over to him. Adrian was suffering from extreme malnourishment and was in a state of hypothermia, but he had no physical injuries, and he was alive.

The servicemen loaded him into the helicopter and carried him away to a hospital. Adrian's week-long ordeal was over.

***

It was four days after he arrived in the hospital that Adrian learned the terrible truth of what had happened to Garrett. Somewhere on his journey back down the river to the boat, the skiff had tipped over into the frigid waters and thrown Garrett in. He'd drowned in the water before he could swim back to shore.

Garrett's body was located 11 days after their hunt, with his body having floated over twenty-two miles away into the mouth of an estuary. The most plausible theory is that they had loaded too much bear meat into the skiff, and somewhere along the journey back, the skiff was unable to hold all the weight and tipped over. Garrett would likely have gone into shock being thrown into the ice-cold water and passed out before drowning.

Commander Pete Melnick, the operations officer of the Coast Guard Air Station in the area, stated that Adrian's experience was "a testament to the human will to live."

It took a while for Adrian to regain his health. He suffered from severe nerve damage, and he also couldn't walk a very long distance without needing to pause to rest. But with the help of professional medical treatment, Adrian slowly began to regain his physical strength. The nerve damage didn't become long-lasting either.

Adrian didn't allow what happened to dissuade him from hunting or venturing out into the woods. On the contrary, he's continued to hunt and spend time outdoors in the years since. In fact, just two months after being stuck out in the Alaskan wilderness, Adrian joined his brother and brother-in-law on a deer hunting trip in Wisconsin.

"I love hunting," said Adrian after the ordeal. "I love the woods. I can't just stop doing the things that I really like in life."

* * *

Let's take a closer look at what happened to hopefully identify what Adrian did right and wrong during his ordeal.

The first mistake that Adrian and Garrett made, and the one that set the whole sequence of tragic events into motion, was simply loading too much bear meat into the skiff. The skiff they used was ridiculously small and only seven feet long, barely large enough to hold the two men and their hunting supplies. But they loaded several hundred pounds of bear meat in an attempt to carry it all back to the boat in just two trips to save time.

The pair should have valued safety over time expediency. They should have reduced the amount of bear meat they transported at once or have used a larger skiff for their transportation.

This wouldn't have guaranteed that the boat wouldn't tip over, but it would have greatly reduced the odds of it happening.

The second major mistake was that Adrian feared the potential presence of bears and wolves more than the tide of the river. That's why he never moved inland up the hills of the island to where it was drier, and he stayed near the river where the tides grew. So much did Adrian fear the bears and wolves, that he hugged the roots of the downed tree by the side of the river when the water rose rather than walk inland.

Adrian may have been weak and physically unprepared to face a bear or a wolf. But he had his rifle with him, and being armed against a bear or wolf was arguably less dangerous than being completely defenseless against the tides of the river. Had the water tides crept up the shoreline just a bit more than they did, Adrian may not have had the strength to get away fast enough. He's extremely lucky he was able to stay just out of range of the water.

The fact that Adrian stayed alive for seven days in the tidal flats is truly astounding but had he moved farther inland he could have stayed dry and potentially even avoided the hypothermia he experienced. For example, he could have moved inland and stayed under spruce or hemlock trees, which would have made him much drier even in the rain.

Adrian stayed out on the tidal flats because he believed it was the most likely location in which he would be found. But he could have moved inland to where it was dryer, taken better shelter, and signaled for help from there.

The other critical mistake Adrian made that likely extended the time he spent out there was that he never made a serious effort to signal for help. While he had difficulty maintaining his fire that he could have used for signaling, he could have ventured a little farther inland where the wood and ground were dryer. There, he could have built another fire and fueled it with green pine boughs to create white smoke in the air and signal for help.

The next major mistake that Adrian made was a lack of communication. The only two people who knew where he was, were Garrett and his wife back home in Michigan. Adrian had informed his wife that he would call her seven days after he and Garrett set out up the river to the island, but he became trapped on the island just four days into those seven days. As a result, his wife had no way of knowing whether Adrian was all right or not.

The fact that Adrian didn't attempt to signal for help and that virtually no one knew he was stranded until several days into his ordeal are the chief reasons why he was stuck out there on that island for as long as he was. Had Adrian done a better job of informing more people of his position beforehand, it's likelier that help would have arrived sooner. For example, Adrian and Garrett could have informed other people back in Ketchikan about where they were going and when to expect their return.

To summarize, the entire incident most likely could have been avoided had Adrian and Garrett simply loaded less meat into their skiff. And even if the tragedy involving Garrett and the skiff could not have been avoided, Adrian could have made wiser choices that would have reduced the time he spent out there while also making the experience a little drier and more bearable for him.

Through it all, however, credit must be given where it is due. It's a miracle Adrian survived, and he endured what would have outright killed most people.

* * *

Just remember one important fact: if you ever find yourself harrowingly stranded out in the wilderness in a situation similar to Adrian's, you can't rely on a miracle to get you out.

By all accounts, Adrian shouldn't have lasted for that week in that inhospitable, frigid, and rain-soaked environment with a lack of food and water.

When you hear 'miracle stories' like Adrian's, and like the others that we have covered thus far, you may think that if you ever find yourself stranded in the wilderness against life-threatening conditions a miracle will come your way too.

But you really can't be too careful. You have to always make sure that you prepare more than adequately when you head out into the wilderness. Always make sure that you bring survival supplies with you, including the ability to create fire, purify water, signal for help, and stay warm. A lighter, water filter, flares, and a survival blanket alone can help keep you alive even in the worst environments on the planet.

That doesn't mean that those are the only items you should bring, but such essential items can make the difference between life and death depending upon your situation.

Next, always make sure that you tell other people where you're going and when they can expect to hear back from you. Ideally, you'll want at least three people to know of the general area you're headed into and when to expect communication or your return.

Remember, for every miracle survival story like Adrian Knopps' or any of the stories we've taken a look at so far, you'll find several more stories of people who *didn't* make it out.

Learn from these true-life stories and try to retain as much of what you learn as you can. If you ever find yourself in a true life-or-death wilderness survival situation, you can think back on these stories and reflect on what their subjects did right and wrong. Keep this in mind as you continue to read on as well.

CHAPTER SIX

BOWHUNTERS VS. BEARS

Two bowhunters, one from California and the other from Ontario, separately found out that black bears can be just as aggressive and dangerous as their grizzly counterparts.

When one thinks of bear attacks, grizzly bears are usually the animal that most comes to mind.

Grizzly bears are much larger and more intimidating than the smaller and seemingly more elusive black bears. Whereas the grizzly bear can regularly attain weights of up to (or over) 1,000 pounds, black bears rarely exceed three hundred pounds.

Furthermore, grizzlies are commonly associated with aggression and are considered a major risk when traveling into the so-called 'grizzly country' in Alaska or Canada. That's why Alaskan hunting guides will regularly carry large-bore handguns to protect their clients against grizzly bear attacks. Black bears, by contrast, are rarely considered a serious threat.

That's because black bears are usually more strongly associated with scavenging and with running away upon encountering humans, whereas grizzly bears are often thought of as natural predators that are more prone to attack.

The reason for the above is that there are indeed far more grizzly attacks than black bear attacks each year. The grizzly has a far more powerful bite force than black bears do, and according to statistics, there are more than twice as many annual grizzly bear attacks on average than attacks from black bears.

But just because grizzly bears are larger and more likely to attack humans than black bears, it does not mean that black bears are not a serious threat in their own right.

Two separate but equally deadly incidents, that both occurred within the last few years serve as poignant reminders that black bears can be just as aggressive and dangerous as their grizzly counterparts. These incidents also serve as lessons about bringing the same level of protection for yourself when venturing out into the black bear country as you do when heading out into the grizzly country.

One of these incidents took place in southern California; the other, the dense woods of Ontario.

* * *

It was bowhunting season for black bears in the San Bernardino mountains in late August 2018. One bowhunter in San Bernadino in 2018 found out the hard way that black bears can be extremely dangerous animals. This hunter, who has remained unnamed since the incident, only barely survived his encounter.

Southern California is most well-known for its massive urban cities like Los Angeles and San Diego. The San Bernardino mountains, however, represent some of the largest areas of true wilderness in the southern part of the state.

These mountains are humid, covered in mixed conifer and pinewood forests, and intersected by crystal clear rivers. The mountains truly represent some of the most beautiful wilderness that the entire state of California has to offer.

There are also an estimated 1,000 adult black bears who inhabit the mountains of San Bernardino, in both San Bernardino and Riverside counties. It's for this reason that the area is considered a prime location for hunting black bears in southern California.

Hunting for black bears with a bow-and-arrow in the San Bernardino mountains takes place in late August and early September. Black bear attacks in this area are incredibly rare, as most confrontations between humans and bears end peacefully with the bear running away.

Not much information exists about the hunter who was severely mauled by a San Bernadino black bear in August 2018, but what we do know serves as a serious reminder that black bears can be among the most dangerous animals in North America when they are provoked.

According to reports, the hunter was one of three who ventured out into the San Bernardino mountains one morning hoping to bag a black bear with his bow and arrow. The names of all three hunters have not been released by the authorities.

After a few hours, the trio of hunters indeed discovered a black bear. One of the hunters aimed with his bow. The arrow flew true and struck the bear in the side, and it went down.

Believing the animal was dead, the hunter approached what he thought was the carcass..., only to realize too late that he had gotten too close to a live bear!

The wounded beast suddenly sprang up and attacked the hunter ferociously, clamping its jaws over his arm and using its claws to inflict deep, grievous wounds into his flesh throughout his body.

Thankfully, the hunter's two companions were present and able to kill the animal with their bows. Had they not been there when the attack happened, the hunter likely would have been killed by the bear outright.

Despite being in critical condition, the hunter and his companions were able to bandage his wounds properly to stop the bleeding, and then they immediately called for help when they returned to an area with cell service. The hunter made it to a hospital, where he miraculously made a full recovery.

There are several important lessons that we can take away from this incident. The first is to never get too close to a bear. Even though this hunter believed the bear was dead when he approached, he let his guard down and it cost him.

The second lesson is to always hunt with at least one partner when you are hunting in bear country, and that goes for black bears just as much as it goes for grizzlies. The hunter in this incident had not just one hunting partner but two, and had it not been for them assisting him in fighting and killing the bear, it's unlikely he could have fought off the animal on his own.

After the attack took place, members of the California Department of Fish and Wildlife went to the site of the attack to inspect the carcass of the bear responsible for the attack. They discovered the bear weighed over three hundred pounds, which was large for a black bear by any standard. The body was later sent to a scientific lab for research.

The hunter in this story was indeed very lucky to escape with his life. It's not the only example of how severe a black bear attack can be either. Next, we'll dive into another story of an aggressive black bear attack that took place in the scenic woodlands of Ontario.

* * *

The second largest province in Canada, Ontario is known for its sprawling woodlands, lakes, and rolling hills that provide hunters with plenty of room to roam around for moose, elk, deer, mountain lions, and black bears.

As in the San Bernardino mountains, black bears are common in the backwoods of Ontario, but attacks on humans are still very rare. One Ontario bowhunter named Richard Wesley was an exception in the spring of 2017.

Wesley was out hunting near Fire River in northeastern Ontario. Coming to a dirt road in an open clearing, surrounded by the woodlands, he suddenly spotted a large black bear a few hundred yards in front of him.

Initially, the bear appeared to completely ignore Wesley as if he wasn't even there. Nonetheless, Wesley loaded an arrow into his bow and aimed at the animal just in case.

Slowly, the bear seemed to take notice of Wesley and moved closer to him but still did not act aggressively. With the bear getting a little too close for comfort, Wesley began making loud noises in an attempt to scare the animal away.

However, making those loud noises may only have served to aggravate the bear rather than the intended effect of intimidating it.

The bear suddenly attacked Wesley head-on. He continued to make loud noises that didn't deter the animal at all. Raising to its two feet, the bear took a major swipe at Wesley, making contact with his elbow. Wesley retaliated by punching the bear in the face and stepping back quickly to avoid further blows from its large paws and claws.

Having captured the entire incident on camera, Wesley released the footage to his YouTube channel, where it has since accumulated more than five million views. The camera was knocked out of Wesley's possession when the bear swiped at him and fell to the ground, so much of the footage is simply of the muddy ground while the sounds of the confrontation can be heard. But what is clearly shown on camera are the moments leading up to the attack as well as when the bear charges Wesley and swipes at him.

Thankfully for Wesley, the bear did not put up much of a fight after that and quickly backed down. As a result, both he and the bear were able to escape the fight without severe injuries, unlike the other hunter we discussed who survived his own black bear attack in San Bernardino.

As Wesley later stated, he was lucky to walk away from the incident with only a "bruised elbow and an ego where the bear threw me down."

He also stated that the attack proved that the black bear, despite normally being considered more docile or non-confrontational than grizzlies, can still be a wild and unpredictable animal. That's precisely why those who are hunting in black bear country need to take the same defensive precautions as when hunting in grizzly country.

When Wesley returned to his log cabin after the incident completely unscathed, he laughed it off. He had just been attacked by a black bear and had gotten away without hardly a single scratch!

But he showed the same footage he would later upload to this YouTube channel to his family. It was only after Wesley witnessed his wife and father's reaction to the video that he realized just how close he had come to losing his life. Had the bear been just a little more aggressive than it was, or if it had gotten a hold of Wesley in its jaws or claws, the outcome would have been far more gruesome.

"We watched the video footage - and my stomach just tightened," Wesley later said. "And my wife started crying."

Wesley's story is a clear indicator that you can never take surviving any animal attack for granted. Had Wesley's family not reminded him of the seriousness of the attack, he may not have taken his own safety as seriously again when he returned to the woods.

CHAPTER SEVEN

ATTACKED BY DOGS

A Georgia hunter discovered that just because hunting season is over doesn't mean the danger is over. When he went back into the woods to take down his tree stand after hunting season had concluded, he found himself brutally attacked by a vicious trio of wolf-like dogs.

Hunters always take a risk when they venture out into the woods on a hunt. Besides the possibility of getting lost or sustaining an injury that leaves them stranded and having to survive against the brutal elements, there's also the danger of being attacked by vicious wild animals.

But as one Georgia hunter named Scott B. discovered in early 2023, the risks of hunting don't end once hunting season is over.

Scott was acutely aware of the inherent risks that hunting always comes with. That's why he always took precautions to protect himself against any potential dangers that could befall him when he was deer hunting in the woods.

He always wore bright orange so other hunters in the area would not mistake him for a deer or another wild animal. He always carried a first aid and survival kit with him just in case he got lost or stranded in the woods. He always attached himself to a safety harness when climbing into his tree stand to avoid the risk of falling out and sustaining a horrific physical injury. And he always carried self-defense weapons to protect himself against the threat of any wild game.

But when Scott returned to the woods after hunting season was over to collect his tree stand, he let his guard down, and the consequences would inflict upon him severe physical and psychological trauma, unlike anything he had ever experienced.

* * *

In mid-January 2023, deer hunting season in Jackson County, Georgia was over. Scott had been hunting for much of his 61-year life, and he had been hunting in this particular area where he had set up his tree stand consistently for seven years. He was remarkably familiar with the area.

It was a typical Sunday morning, and Scott decided that he would move the tree stand he used for hunting in his typical hunting area to another spot in preparation for next year. He also figured that he would take advantage of this opportunity to go for a nice walk in the woods.

The possibility of finding himself in any danger was the very last thing on his mind. Scott would take his time enjoying a relaxing morning walk in the woods, move the tree stand, and then be on his merry way. At least that was the plan.

Little did Scott know, but he would soon find himself in the most traumatic life-or-death struggle of his life.

At first, everything went according to plan. Scott woke up early, had his breakfast and coffee, and then set off to the site of his ladder stand in his ATV. Disembarking from the vehicle, he walked over 150 yards through the woods to the tree stand. He was unarmed.

Arriving at the site of the tree stand, Scott began to undo the ladder from around the trunk of the tree. He had decided that he would move the stand to another tree around 150 yards away, believing that the new location would provide him with a better vantage point during next season's deer hunt.

It was then that, out of the corner of his eye, he spotted three dogs materializing out of the woods into the clearing.

Two of the dogs were pit-bull mixes, and the third was a German Shepherd mix. They looked just like the kinds of dogs that you'd expect to see people walking at the dog park and hardly seemed threatening..., at least at first.

"They had apparently been attracted to the noise I was making in the woods," Scott later recalled.

Scott didn't know where the dogs had come from or who they belonged to, but he continued with his work of tearing down the tree stand. But the more the dogs watched him, the more uneasy he started to get.

Suddenly, one of the dogs burst forward and charged Scott directly! There was no time for Scott to react. The animal's jaws clamped over his leg and twisted. Scott screamed and tried to fight off the dog, but it released its jaws only to bite down hard again.

The other two dogs, triggered by the actions of the first animal, charged forward and joined in on the attack. Now Scott had the jaws of all three dogs over him, diving their fangs deep into his legs, arms, hips, and torso.

The pain was excruciating beyond belief. But Scott had to believe that he could get away because that was the only way he was going to survive this freak encounter with these vicious canines from hell.

Scott screamed for help, but no one was in the general vicinity who could help him. He had also left his phone in his ATV, which he had parked over 150 yards away from the scene of the attack. There was no one there to help him, and there was no way that he could find help from anyone either.

And he was unarmed.

Where's the pepper spray? Scott asked himself as he attempted to fight off the animals. *Where's my revolver?*

Was Scott losing his mind or just his flesh? He'd grab one dog that had its jaws locked around his legs and rip it away from him, only for another dog to latch onto another part of his body.

The dogs were biting him repeatedly all over his body, their teeth puncturing from the skin to the bone. But even amid the attack, Scott stayed smart. He knew that his neck and the arteries in his legs were his most vulnerable, and he attempted to shield these areas from attack the most.

"They were attacking me from all sides," Scott later said of the incident. "It was kind of like a wolf mentality. I was trying to keep them away from the inside of my negs where the femoral arteries are and away from my neck."

Deciding he needed to fight back instead of just attempting to get the animals off of him, Scott picked up a large stick on the ground and began to whack it against the dogs. Finally, the dogs began to relent and back off. With their ears back and fangs bared, they growled at Scott as he backed up, still shouting at the top of his lungs and swinging the big stick back and forth to keep them away.

Scott knew he had to get away from the dogs before they ripped him to shreds, and he knew that the option was to climb up his tree stand. But he was unable to climb his own tree stand because he had loosened it to take it down, so there was no use in trying to climb it.

Instead, he began to walk slowly towards another ladder stand that he knew was on a nearby piece of property, keeping a close eye on all three of the animals as they circled him. His movements were hindered by the deep wounds his legs had sustained, which were flowing with blood.

Each time the dogs charged forward again - Scott would strike them with the stick. He realized that whacking them over their thick skulls had insignificant effect, so he whacked the stick over their backs and sides instead. The pain that each whack inflicted upon the dogs caused them to yelp and keep back for a moment, giving Scott temporary relief.

Scott considered doing what he had heard you should do in a bear attack, which was fall to the ground and roll up in a ball to act dead, but he decided that this plan would be too difficult against three dogs attacking him from all angles at once. Continuing to defend with his stick while backing up to the nearby tree stand was his safest bet - but he had to do it before he would pass out from blood loss.

Finally reaching the stand, Scott hastily climbed up the ladder steps to the elevated platform, escaping the sharp teeth of the merciless animals.

"They were still biting me, but spinning with that stick kept them from teaming up and keeping me stuck in one place," he recalled. "As I was going up the ladder stand, I told myself that I really needed to hold on tight to the rungs because the dogs are going to be jumping on my backside and trying to pull me down - and if they did, I'd probably never get away."

Atop the stand, Scott was able to catch his breath and take a look over his injuries. He could instantly see that he was in horrific shape, for deep lacerations and punctures had ripped apart his arms from shoulders to hands and his legs from waist to ankles. Blood was flowing profusely, and if he were unable to stop the bleeding soon, he knew he would pass out.

The dogs remained on the ground beneath the stand, but slowly they began to lose interest. Eventually, they turned and disappeared back into the woods in the same direction they had come from.

Scott still took no chances. He stayed in the stand for 30 minutes, attempting to stop the bleeding with his clothing and taking his time to ensure the dogs had left for good.

When he slowly began to descend the ladder, knowing he needed to seek medical attention immediately, the fallen leaves on the ground rustled when he stepped over them. It was only a matter of seconds before all three of the dogs came bursting out of the trees again.

Immediately, Scott turned and quickly scurried back up the ladder, barely avoiding the razor-sharp fangs of the dogs. They barked and hissed and growled, eager for him to descend from the platform again so they could finish their deadly work, but again Scott stayed patient.

Again, the dogs slowly began to lose interest and disappeared back into the forest, and again, Scott waited the entirety of half an hour before taking the risk to descend from the platform again.

This time, Scott yelled at the top of his lungs to see if the dogs would reemerge. To his relief, they did not.

Even though Scott was just 150 yards away from his ATV, he decided to head in the opposite direction. The dogs had originally come from the same direction as his ATV, and he didn't want to take the chance that he would encounter them again before reaching it. He was severely weakened and losing blood, and if he ran into the dogs again there would be no tree stand that he could escape to this time. His only hope now was to head in the opposite direction of his ATV, his only mode of transportation, and pray he wouldn't run into the dogs again before finding help.

* * *

Struggling to walk from the deep and bloody lacerations that crisscrossed his legs, Scott eventually came to a fence line about sixty yards away. He managed to climb over the fence and then pushed on through the woods before coming to an open cow pasture. He stumbled across the pasture to a highway on the other side.

To Scott's disbelief, not one of the vehicles driving past him pulled over for quite some time.

"I stood in the middle of the road waving my arms and people were driving around me!" Scott later reported. "I knew I looked like hell, but dang, a couple of guys all alone in pickup trucks drove around me. You'd think they could have stopped at a distance, rolled down the window and asked if I needed help. It was obvious I needed medical attention."

Finally, one vehicle slowed down and pulled over to the side of the road. Scott quickly explained what had happened and that he needed to get to a medical emergency room as soon as possible. It just so happened that the vehicle he had pulled over was a family on their way to church that Sunday, but they wasted no time in letting Scott into the vehicle and flooring it to the nearest hospital as fast as they could.

At the hospital, Scott learned from the doctors who operated on him that he had no less than 298 puncture wounds, cuts, and lacerations all over his body. A ligament in his hand was badly torn as well. He was sewn up with dozens of stitches in seven separate places in his body. The lacerations he had sustained would turn into scars that he would have had for the rest of his life, but he was alive.

After being treated for his wounds, Scott made his way to the local police station where he filed a police report. The police contacted the local animal control unit and reported the incident. Traveling to the site of the attack, the animal control officers were able to track down the animals at the nearby home at which they lived. All three of the dogs were confiscated and the owner was fined for the possession of dangerous animals.

The three dogs were then kept in mandatory quarantine for 10 days to confirm they didn't have rabies before being euthanized.

* * *

Scott faced a long road to recovery, but he was immensely grateful for this survival. His legs had become so badly swollen after the attack, that he was forced to wear compression sleeves for three weeks. He then turned to physical therapy to regain his full range of motion.

The experience was incredibly traumatic for Scott, and he initially questioned whether he would return to the woods again. He admitted that the attack left a severe mental and psychological impact on him and that he couldn't return to the woods without reliving what had happened, but eventually, he started to go on hikes in the woods again with his family members.

Nonetheless, Scott reflected on what had happened to identify the mistakes he had made and how he could avoid them in future. He has since decided that he would never go hunting again without additional hunters within his party.

He also decided that he would always carry self-defense weapons each time he ventured out into the woods. One of

Scott's mistakes was leaving his weapons at home rather than bringing them with him. He had left his weapons because he had thought he wouldn't find himself in a situation where he would need them. He now carries a handgun, a collapsible steel baton, and a bear spray canister each time he ventures out into the woods, regardless of whether he goes alone or with other people.

The incident Scott experienced goes to show the importance of always arming yourself before heading out into the woods or wilderness.

It's also worth noting that Scott did several things right during his ordeal. Even though he let his guard down by heading out into the woods unarmed, when the dogs attacked him, he protected the arteries of his inner legs and his neck as much as possible because these were the most vulnerable points of his body. Had any of the dogs clamped their jaws around his inner legs or his neck and ripped open his arteries, Scott likely would have bled out and died.

Scott also took action to arm himself with the natural resources at his disposal. He picked up a large stick from the ground and used it to beat back against the animals, evening the odds and helping to shield himself from further attack.

Furthermore, Scott was able to escape up a tree stand to escape the dogs. Even while he was being attacked, he remembered the nearby tree standing on the adjacent piece of property. He made his way over to it and, despite the continued attacks, managed to climb up the ladder and evade the animals. Had Scott not been able to escape up the tree stand, then the dogs would likely have kept on attacking him rather than losing interest and going away.

Scott's experience teaches us three particularly important lessons to remember during any animal attack: always protect the most vulnerable parts of your body; always try to arm yourself with something around you if you have no weapons on you; and always try to escape to higher ground so you can get away.

This doesn't just apply to hunters. It applies to anyone who goes for a walk in the woods as well because you never know what kind of dangerous animals you're going to encounter. As Scott's experience has proven, it's not just wild animals like bears or wolves that can be a threat. Domesticated dogs can be a threat too if they're not friendly and in the right mood to attack.

CHAPTER EIGHT

FIVE DAYS IN THE BACKWOODS OF TENNESSEE

A squirrel hunter who got separated from his hunting partners became stranded alone in the Tennessee wilderness. Over the ensuing five days, he lived off of a diet of worms and muddy water to survive.

The backwoods of Tennessee are not exactly what comes to mind when you think of a pleasant place in which to be stranded.

Meeman-Shelby Forest State Park is no exception, a sprawling 13,000-acre landscape of dense oak and hickory trees, rivers, swamps, and muddy terrain. It's the most popular state park in Tennessee, attracting thousands of people a year who come for boating, biking, camping, hiking, and hunting.

But finding yourself stranded in Meeman-Shelby would be no walk in the park, as one man by the name of Bill Lawrence found out in 2011.

Bill was a Corrections Officer who worked at the Tipton County Sheriff's Office in Tennessee. He was also an avid outdoorsman, and he spent much of his free time with his friends in Tennessee's outdoor areas. For all of his life, Meeman-Shelby was an outdoor haven for Bill, as it had been for countless other people, and he enjoyed going to the park to hunt for small game.

But as Bill would soon find out, the backwoods of Meeman-Shelby would throw at him the biggest challenge for survival he would ever face.

It was late August in 2011, and Bill ventured into the woods of Meeman-Shelby with two of his friends to embark on one of his favorite recreational hunting activities: squirrel hunting.

But the woods of Meeman-Shelby are very dense, and it's easy to get lost. Bill would soon fall victim to the same simple and yet very dangerous hazard that had befallen so many others before him - getting lost in the woods.

Bill was stepping through the dense foliage, flanked by his friends on both sides of him. The three of them stayed quiet; the leaves crunching under the boots and the shots of other hunters in the area echoing in the distance were the only noises they could hear.

Bill sighted a squirrel, but the little furry animal scurried away into the underbrush before Bill could bring his shotgun to his shoulder.

Quickly, perhaps a little too quickly, Bill took off after the squirrel. He figured he'd find it, shoot it, and then bring it back to show off to his two other friends.

"I'll be right back," Bill told his friends.

* * *

Well, that's not exactly how things panned out. Bill chased after the squirrel, but he was unable to locate it no matter how hard he looked. He peered up trees, looked through the underbrush, and kept walking for some distance, but his elusive quarry had evaded him.

Finally, Bill gave up the chance and elected to turn around and return to his friends.

He walked - and walked and walked. The woods and foliage were like a maze, and everything looked the same no matter where you walked or how far you went.

When Bill thought he had walked as far as he had gone and still had no sight of his friends, he began to get worried. He called out for them, but no one answered.

He kept walking and kept calling. Nothing but the silence of the woods.

Then Bill realized that he could no longer hear the noise of distant shots from other hunters shooting like he and his friends had been hearing all morning long. Had he really walked off that far?

Bill raised his shotgun to his shoulder and fired off two shots in rapid succession. If either of his friends or any other hunters in the area heard the report of the gun, they'd fire back two shots in rapid succession as well. Then Bill could walk in the direction of where the shots were coming from.

His heart sank as he waited for the report of two other shotgun blasts in the distance, but there were none.

Bill gave up trying to find his friends and decided he'd walk back to the area where they had parked their truck. Then he would wait for them to come back out of the woods and reunite with them.

He walked for hours through the forest in the direction he thought they had parked the truck, but yet again, it was all in vain. There were just more trees and more brush everywhere he walked and looked.

It started to get chilly as the afternoon was slowly turning into evening. Bill had no cell or internet service and therefore no way of contacting help or the outside world. He had lost his friends and he could no longer recollect exactly where the truck was.

Slowly, it dawned upon Bill that he had become lost and stranded in the middle of the forest and that he would need to spend the night there.

It couldn't be that difficult, he figured. He had spent countless nights camping out in the woods growing up and in his adult life, and this would be no different. The only difference is he would be on his own and have fewer resources at his disposal. If he could get a good night's sleep, he could hopefully figure out where the parking lot was and resume walking in the morning.

Bill took inventory of the items he had available. Besides the camouflage hunting clothes and the snake boots he was wearing, he had his shotgun, fifteen shells of ammunition, two water bottles, a flashlight, a squirrel call, a can of dip, and a can of bug spray.

That was certainly better than having nothing at all, but there were many items that Bill was wishing he had: namely food, a fire starter, and a survival blanket. Each of these would have made him feel a little more comfortable. At least his shotgun could be used for self-defense against dangerous game animals or to signal for help, he thought.

* * *

Bill didn't know it, but his friends had spent hours searching for him. They'd called out for him and fired their shotguns in the air, but they'd got no response.

With no other options, they'd returned to their truck and waited for hours hoping that Bill would meet up with them there. When he never did, they'd wasted no time in reporting him as missing.

In a matter of hours, search and rescue teams were on the ground and sweeping all over Meeman-Shelby Forest State Park looking for Bill. Searchers rode ATVs and horses through the forests, led trained dog teams, drove boats up and down rivers, and scoured the thick woods from above in helicopters.

But the helicopters could hardly see anything through the dense canopy of the trees.

* * *

When it rains in Tennessee, it pours. Bill took as much cover as he could under the trees while collecting rainwater in his hunting vest.

When the rain let up, he pressed on walking through the woods. The ground had become very muddy, making it difficult to keep up a brisk pace. His feet became wet as water seeped through his boots.

Over the next four days, Bill suffered from extreme thirst and hunger. When his water bottles and the rainwater he had collected ran out, he drank water from the muddy puddles on the ground. He had no choice.

When he could no longer walk without great difficulty due to a lack of calories and energy, he dug into the mud with his fingers and found earthworms.

For the first time in his life, worms actually looked appetizing. With no way of building a fire, Bill ate them raw.

"I saw it on TV," he later said when recounting the incident.

The worms tasted gross, but they gave Bill the energy he needed to continue.

Another threat to Bill was the scorching heat and the never-ending mosquitoes that started to overwhelm him after he ran out of his bug spray. It may pour when it rains in Tennessee, but when it gets hot, it gets sweltering. Bill stopped walking often to take cover under the trees for shade before continuing and to keep himself hydrated, he continued drinking water out of muddy puddles.

Each time Bill thought he heard somebody, he fired his shotgun into the air to try and alert them. By Saturday, the fourth day, he had run out of shells.

This was Bill's life for five days. Stumbling through the dense Tennessee woods, swatting flies and mosquitoes that pestered his skin, eating earthworms to keep his energy going, and drinking mud to stay hydrated.

On Sunday, the fifth day, Bill finally staggered out onto a road. Amazingly, it was only three miles away from where he had originally started. That was because Bill had walked over thirty-five miles just walking around in circles!

He was dehydrated and he was covered in bug bites, but he was alive. Two motorcycle riders pulled up alongside the ragged and barely alive man and took him in.

* * *

Bill didn't know it, but the search for him was major local news. Almost immediately upon his discovery, he was taken to a press conference where the authorities announced his survival.

Too weak to speak to reporters at the press conference, Bill went to Methodist North Hospital where he was provided treatment for his bug bites and given food and water.

When news broke out that Bill had been located, family, friends, and search volunteers poured into the hospital.

"We hugged and I kissed him all over his face," his mother, Denise, recalled. "I just couldn't keep my hands off of him."

Afterwards, Bill released a statement from the Tipton County Sheriff's Office at which he worked.

"I would like to start by thanking the good Lord above, without him I would not have made it out alive," he said.

* * *

There are many lessons that we can learn from Bill's ordeal. The first one is to always know your sense of direction when you go hunting or for a walk out in the woods. This is easier said than done on your own in the maze of the woods, so always bring a GPS with you that can inform you of your current location.

It was also because of this lack of direction that Bill wasted precious time and energy walking around in circles. Even though he had physically walked more than thirty-five miles, he ended up only covering three miles of distance. Had he merely walked three miles out from where he was in a straight line, Bill would have come to the road (and help) far sooner than he had, and he could have avoided the whole ordeal.

It's also important to always bring food with you when you venture out into the wilderness; even simple granola bars or candy in your pockets are better than having nothing at all. If Bill had brought food with him, he probably could have avoided having to eat worms.

But through it all, Bill did a few things right from which we can learn. Most notably, he remained calm and collected, and remained focused on his priorities. He knew he needed food and water and actively searched for sources, while also giving his body plenty of rest so he didn't get exhausted too quickly.

"I just tried to remain calm, get as much rest as I could, and try to find a water source and something to eat," said Bill of the experience later. "The water source was nasty, and I was drinking muddy water, but I drank it."

The worms and the muddy water may have tasted nasty, but they kept Bill hydrated and energized just enough for him to persist. Had he avoided these, Bill may not have had the energy he needed to continue walking, and the search and rescue teams may have never found him.

Drinking muddy water or eating grubs is always a risk due to the possibility of bacteria and infections setting in, but thankfully, Bill was able to receive the proper medical treatment after.

All in all, Bill's story is a classic reminder of the old adage "Don't get lost."

But if you do get lost, stay calm and push on.

CHAPTER NINE

THE SPEAR FISHERMAN AND THE SHARK

A 70-year-old spear fisherman got more than he bargained for when he became the victim of a brutal bull shark attack off the coast of Florida.

Most of the survival stories we've covered so far occurred on land.

But what about beneath the depths of the ocean?

In many ways, the ocean is a more terrifying place than land. This is because the ocean is inherently a more mysterious place than land. We don't know everything that's down there, and what we do know is that there's a very real risk of drowning in the event you find yourself left behind and stranded out in the ocean all on your own.

And even if you don't drown, many deadly sea creatures lurk under the depths that will kill you. The one sea creature that has perhaps generated more fear in the hearts and minds of people than any other is the shark.

But surprisingly enough, there aren't very many recorded shark attacks worldwide. There is an average of seventy shark attacks each year, which isn't very many when you consider that hundreds of millions of people swim each year in waters inhabited by sharks.

And of those seventy attacks per year, only five people die. The rest have escaped with their lives, albeit usually with grievous and life-altering wounds.

The very fact that shark attacks are so few and far between is why they almost always make the news and attract national or global media attention, and this creates the impression that shark attacks are a very common event.

None of this is to doubt or call into question the severity of shark attacks when they occur or to say that you shouldn't take safety precautions when you go swimming or fishing in the ocean.

But when shark attacks do happen, they often happen due to people not taking the proper safety precautions. If you are warned that any area you are considering swimming in is known for having sharks nearby, don't take the chance. Sometimes, however, it doesn't matter how many safety precautions you take…

Also, perhaps surprisingly enough, the most dangerous sharks (or the sharks that are involved in the most shark attacks each year) are not the most famous, like great white sharks or tiger sharks.

Rather, the most dangerous shark in the world and the one that is involved in the most shark attacks is the bull shark.

Bull sharks are considerably smaller than great white and tiger sharks, but that doesn't make them any less dangerous. Bull sharks specifically are involved in the most shark attacks because they usually inhabit the shallower waters that people go swimming or fishing in; larger species of sharks like the great white or tiger shark usually inhabit deeper waters.

Furthermore, bull sharks are a euryhaline-type of shark, meaning they can survive in both fresh and saltwater. As a result, bull sharks have been known to swim all the way up freshwater rivers, hundreds of miles away from the ocean; many have been sighted in the Mississippi River in the United States and in the Ganges River in India, to name a few examples.

This survival story we are about to dive into, however, takes place off the coast of Florida. Bull sharks are among the apex predators in Florida's waters. Although shark attacks may be infrequent, you can't be too careful when fishing or swimming in areas known to be inhabited by sharks.

One man named Rick Neuman found this out in April 2015.

* * *

Rick was no stranger to the ocean. He was a spear fisherman for over 55 years of his 70-year life, but even in his older years, he had the same zeal and enthusiasm for the sport of spearfishing as he originally had as a young man.

One day, he set out with others on a 20-foot boat off the coast of Palm Beach, Florida. Dressed in a hooded wetsuit and armed with a speargun, Rick was well-prepared for what was supposed to be another fun day of spearfishing.

The boat was more than three miles from the shoreline, and the temperature of the water was a very warm 78 degrees Fahrenheit.

The water was slightly murky, but Rick still had around five to twenty feet of visibility when he peered into the water under the boat.

The total depth of the water below the boat was around fifty feet, which was considerably shallow considering the average depth of the ocean is around 12,000 feet…, but it still wasn't shallow enough for bull sharks.

Rick's friend Julian dived into the water first. When he resurfaced, he revealed that he had caught a big prize in the form of a 50-pound cobia fish.

Encouraged by his friend's success, Rick dove into the murky water next. He had on his wetsuit, but he wasn't using scuba gear.

As Rick was underwater, Julian and his other friends waited patiently for him on the boat. Rick resurfaced, revealing he had caught a hog snapper to the congratulations of his friends.

He elected to dive one more time before returning to the boat. Diving into the murky waters again, Rick suddenly caught sight of something that caused his heart to nearly stop: the tail fin of a shark.

Slowly, a seven-foot bull shark came into his view.

Rick froze. He knew from his 55 years of experience that the most important thing to do when you encounter a shark in the water is to stay still. Sharks are naturally attracted to movement, and Rick knew that even the slightest movement would be enough to attract the attention of the shark.

It's a terribly similar strategy to that of curling up and lying still on the ground to act dead when you encounter a grizzly bear in the woods.

For a moment, the shark remained still as well. Rick's heart was pounding. If only the shark would continue to swim on its way…

Suddenly, the shark came hurling forward directly toward Rick with its jaws open!

Rick instinctively reacted. He raised his spear gun and stuck the spear deep into the mouth of the shark. The jaws of the mighty animal bit down upon it, breaking it nearly in half.

Rick began swimming furiously for the surface.

But the shark wasn't done with him yet.

The beast moved forward and clamped its jaws around Rick's fin. Again, Rick counterattacked with his spear gun, stabbing the shark directly in the nose.

Again, Rick's experience and instincts came into play here. He knew the best strategy with a shark was to play dead and move still. But if a shark attacked, the next best strategy was to stab it in the place it hated to be attacked the most: the nose.

But that only made the shark more infuriated than it already was. Managing to twist its way free of Rick's spear gun, it lurched forward again and sank its many rows of razor-sharp teeth deep into Rick's shoulder, neck, and ear.

"The next thing I know, something slams into my head and right shoulder," Rick recalled after the event, "and I mean hard. It knocked my mask off. I turned and saw him swimming away. I probably dove right on top of him, and he was showing me who was boss in his kingdom down there."

Rick would have screamed had he not been underwater. The jaws of the shark ripped his diving mask from his face and part of his left ear from the side of his head.

Finally, the shark released its grip on Rick. By now, Rick knew, fighting against the shark was hopeless. His only chance of survival was to swim furiously for the surface and get back in the boat and pray that the shark would not attack him again.

* * *

Rick made it back to the surface where he thrashed about and screamed for help. His alarmed friends wasted no time in hauling him back up onto the boat.

Rick had sustained severe lacerations to his right shoulder, his neck, and his ear. His flesh was ripped open, and he was bleeding profusely. His friends were horrified, but they wasted no time.

Patching up Rick as best they could to stop the flow of bleeding, the members of the crew made a call to the emergency rescue services while hightailing the boat at high speeds back to shore.

Within 40 minutes, the boat was docked at the U-Tiki Beach restaurant in Jupiter Inlet. Emergency medical responders were there waiting for them.

Rick was quickly airlifted by helicopter to the St Mary's Medical Center, located in West Palm Beach, where the doctors immediately went to work to save his life.

He ended up having more than two sutures and staples to close up his open wounds, and a part of his ear had to be reattached as well. But he made a full recovery.

Through it all, Rick didn't blame the shark.

Rick suspected after the attack that the bull shark that attacked him was hunting for the same cobia fish that he and his friends were spearfishing for and that the shark may have even attacked him by mistake. As a result, he bore no feelings of ill will for the animal and expressed no desire to return to the site of the incident in an attempt to hunt it down for revenge.

"He bit through the wet suit, and part of me, then realized neither one was a fish and just went on his way," Rick recollected. "I think the shark got confused and just lashed out and hit me like a freight train on the right side of my shoulder and head."

He also expressed no fear about returning to the ocean.

"The water was dirty, and things can happen," Rick said.

* * *

What can we learn from Rick's experience?

Perhaps the most important thing is to keep your calm.

Rick's experience also proved to be an asset. He knew to always stay calm and still around a shark when you encounter one in the water, and this was instinctively the first thing he did. He also knew that the most effective place to strike a shark is on the nose, and that's what he did with his spear.

Through it all, Rick never panicked and did exactly as he was supposed to do.

Still, Rick was also very lucky. When the shark released its grip on his neck and shoulder, it didn't attack him again. If it had, the outcome may have been far more tragic than it ended up being.

As we discussed before, shark attacks are rare but when they happen, they are unexpected, quick, and brutal. Trapped in the shark's jaws beneath the surface of the water where you can't breathe, you are completely at the mercy of the shark.

Rick was lucky. If the shark had kept him underwater just a few moments longer, he could have drowned.

Rick's experience is a prime example that you can never be too careful when you're spending time out in the sea. Even if it's not a shark that gets to you, you never know what else could be lurking under the waters…

CHAPTER TEN

31 DAYS IN THE AMAZON

This is the true story of a Bolivian hunter who became separated from his party while on a hunting trip deep in the Amazon Rainforest. Armed with only a shotgun with one round, he was forced to survive more than a month in the jungle by eating bugs and drinking his own urine, all while facing off against jaguars, wild pigs, and an assortment of venomous creatures.

There is arguably no harder place to survive in the world than in the Amazon rainforest.

This enormous jungle covers over a billion acres throughout Brazil, Colombia, Ecuador, Peru, and Venezuela. Flying above the green canopy, you'll look down upon a lush, tropical paradise that spans across the horizon seemingly forever.

But it's beneath the tops of the trees and deep into the thick undergrowth that the Amazon truly begins to show its true beauty. This rainforest is one of the most biodiverse places on the planet and is home to more than two million species of insects, 2,500 species of trees, and thousands of species of mammals, reptiles, and amphibians. There are plants and creatures of all shapes, sizes, and colors in the Amazon, and many of the plants and creatures there do not exist anywhere else in the world.

It's also beneath the tops of the trees that the Amazon begins to show its ugly and harrowing side as well. Find yourself stranded somewhere in the remote and dense maze of trees and vines and brush, and you'll have many miles of walking to do to get back to civilization.

The undergrowth of the Amazon is also very thick and makes walking at great distances with ease difficult. You'll find yourself tangled in dangling vines, slogging through wet mud, and attempting to cross raging rivers without getting swept away. Much of the trees, roots, vines, and brush in the Amazon are grouped so closely together that they look the same no matter where you walk, so it's quite easy to end up walking around in circles and wasting precious time and energy.

The Amazon is one of the wettest and most humid places in the world as well. With nine feet of rainfall a year, during the wet season, your boots or shoes will hardly ever be in contact with dry ground, and you'll barely have any respite from the shower of water from above. When it rains at night then you'll be soaked to the skin with no way of avoiding the downfall of rain, and when it doesn't rain at night, you'll become the victim of dozens if not hundreds of individual bug bites all over your body. You'll then be forced to continue during the day, exhausted from the lack of sleep.

Then there's the fact that most of the thousands of types of creatures who inhabit this lush paradise will try to kill you. If any of the millions of species of venomous insects and frogs in the Amazon don't kill you in your sleep, you may find yourself in the fangs and claws of a jaguar, wrapped in the restrictive embrace of a boa constrictor or Anaconda, or shredded apart by piranhas while attempting to cross a river.

If you find yourself stranded in the Amazon, you'll be at the mercy of the rainforest itself and the millions of deadly creatures who inhabit this lost world. Surviving here and making it out alive requires having the right skills and knowledge…, with that, maybe a little bit of luck.

Making it out even after just three days alone in the Amazon would be a miracle, let alone a week. The chances of you surviving here on your own without supplies alone for a month would be very remote…but not impossible.

* * *

Jhonattan Acosta was no stranger to the Amazon Rainforest. A 30-year-old man who had grown up in Bolivia, he had spent much time hiking, camping, exploring, and hunting in the dense undergrowth of the jungle.

It was January 2023, and Jhonattan was embarking on another hunting trip with his friends in the part of the Amazon that stretched into northern Bolivia.

They went into the jungle to go bird hunting. Jhonattan was armed with a shotgun and a machete, and he carried a flashlight with him as well. During a break with his friends, he set the machete and flashlight down, and they were picked up by someone else. Jhonattan then picked up his shotgun as they got up and headed out into the thick undergrowth again.

Less weighed down now that he was carrying fewer supplies, Jhonattan began to walk ahead of the group. His mind became transfixed by the beauty of the jungle, with the rays of the sun shining through the leaves of the green canopy above him, the massive roots jutting out of the ground that he was careful to step over, and the web of vines that wrapped around and dangled from trees.

Jhonattan mentally escaped during his extended moment of hypnotic bliss and stopped walking. Eventually, he turned around to spot where his friends were. He couldn't see them.

He waited a bit, hoping they would catch up and reappear through the trees and vines again, but they never did. He yelled out, hoping to hear a callback, but no one answered.

Befuddled, Jhonattan began to make his way back in the direction he had come. But everywhere he looked, everything looked the same. All the trees, all the vines, all the plants sticking out of the muddy ground, the canopy overhead….

His heart rate began to accelerate. He no longer recognized where he was. He called out again and again in the humid air for his friends as loud as he could, but he heard nothing other than the buzzing of the insects and birds around him.

Slowly, it dawned upon Jhonattan that he had walked too far from his friends and that he was now officially separated from them.

He had left most of his supplies with his friends, including his water, his machete, and a flashlight. The only tool he had with him was his shotgun…, with only one round.

* * *

For the first four days of his ordeal, Jhonattan remained hopeful. He was confident that his friends, upon realizing he was gone, would immediately contact the authorities who would then search and rescue teams after him. His friends knew the general vicinity of where he was, so the teams would know where to look, he thought.

But having hope doesn't mean he was having an easy time. Still, Jhonattan managed to feed himself with a papaya-like fruit he found, as he knew it was safe to eat as he had eaten the same fruit before (the specific fruit was referred to as a 'gargarteas' by the locals).

It started to rain heavily, and even though he didn't have a canteen, he was able to use his rubber boots to collect and drink the rainwater.

"I asked God for rain," Acosta later recounted, "if it hadn't rained, I would not have survived."

On the fourth day, Jhonattan realized that since no one had found him, his only chance of survival was to walk out. But while on the move, he tripped and fell over a big root that jutted out of the ground. When he attempted to get back up, he realized that his ankle was out of joint and dislocated.

It was at this moment that Jhonattan began to think that he wouldn't make it out alive. The search and rescue teams hadn't found him yet, and now his mobility was severely restricted.

He couldn't walk on his own two feet, so he had to use an extended stick as a makeshift walking stick.

It stopped raining, and Jhonattan had drunk all of the water he had collected in his rubber boots. When he became so thirsty to the point that he could not go on, he drank the water he found in muddy pools and his own urine. He ate insects and worms to keep his energy up; walking was an even greater ordeal and required more energy now due to his twisted ankle, so Jhonattan needed all the protein he could get to keep moving.

Another problem was the never-ending pestering from bugs and insects. Jhonattan would wake up each morning to dozens of new bug bites, and he constantly had to be on his guard to avoid the snakes and spiders that were crawling on the ground and the trees.

"It helped a lot to know about survival techniques," Jhonattan later recalled, "I had to consume insects, drink my urine, and eat worms. I was attacked by animals."

One night while attempting to sleep against a tree, Jhonattan encountered a group of wild pigs who took an interest in him. When they got too close and showed no sign of backing off, Jhonattan fired the one shell in his shotgun at them. They scattered back into the trees.

One day it started to rain again, and Jhonattan was able to collect and drink the clean water. This gave him a renewed feeling of hope. He also continued to hold out hope that search and rescue parties were still out looking for him.

On another day, Jhonattan caught sight of the black and tan spotted hide of a jaguar that was slinking through the undergrowth. Even though he had already spent his one shot against the wild pigs, Jhonattan thought he could still use the shotgun as a club if the big cat came too close. Thankfully the jaguar never did, but for the rest of his ordeal, Jhonattan had to assume that he was being stalked by the beast as he was in its vicinity.

On the 31st day of his ordeal, Jhonattan was continuing to make his way through the jungle when he suddenly stopped at what he thought were voices in the air. His mind had to be playing tricks on him, he thought.

But slowly the voices got louder and louder. Jhonattan's heart began to race, but this time, it was out of excitement and relief and not out of desperation like it was before. Then the moving, colored shirts of people began to materialize out of the brown and green undergrowth.

Jhonattan immediately called out to them. He staggered as fast as he could, and when they heard and saw him, they ran up to him.

He collapsed into their arms as they met in the middle, and he cried tears of joy at his disbelief at being found.

Jhonattan had been rescued.

* * *

Jhonattan's belief that the search and rescue teams were out searching for him had turned out to be correct. In fact, it was a search and rescue team looking for him that he had happened to stagger upon. The search and rescue teams had even used a specially trained dog called Titan to help search for him.

Throughout his time alone in the Amazon, Jhonattan never thought that he could walk back to civilization. Rather, he was counting on being found by people out looking for him, and this hope was what kept him going. His hopes turned out to be reality. He was surprised to realize that they had kept the search going for him for over a month.

At first, the members of the search party thought that Jhonattan was another searcher. But when they saw how bad a shape he was in, they quickly realized that they had found the missing man.

Spiritually re-energized by the experience, Jhonattan decided to dedicate the rest of his life to creating music for God.

"I thank God profusely because he has given me a new life," Jhonattan said after his rescue.

He had lost forty pounds, suffered a dislocated ankle, and was covered in scrapes and cuts and bug bites, but Jhonattan had survived.

* * *

The truth is that we know little of the specific details of Jhonattan's ordeal because very little information has been released. What we do know was what was reported by media outlets in the days following his rescue. Everything that we currently know is what is recounted above.

But there's still a lot we can learn from what happened. Jhonattan survived in the Amazon for 31 days, which makes him one of the longest-ever recorded lone survivors in the Amazon. Furthermore, he accomplished this feat with nothing more than a shotgun and one shell, and after suffering a dislocated ankle that slowed down his movement. So, Jhonattan did a few things right to get him out.

The first thing Jhonattan did right was to collect rainwater. Even though he didn't have a canteen or a bottle with him, he took off his rubber boots and used those to collect and carry the water with him. This kept him hydrated for several days.

And when it stopped raining and the water, he collected in his boots ran out, Jhonattan resorted to drinking the water he saw in muddy pools and even his own urine. Even though it wasn't pleasant and carried the risk of becoming seriously infected with bacteria, the alternative was not drinking anything.

It only takes one day without water for the human body to become severely dehydrated and three days before death. Jhonattan was acutely that he was faced with the risk of drinking urine and contaminated water versus the certainty of death, and he chose the former.

Jhonattan was also able to use his knowledge of plants and fruits to determine which ones were safe to drink. This was due to his experiences spending time in the jungle growing up and in his young adulthood.

Jhonattan used the right combination of skills, knowledge, and determination to make it out. Throughout the 31 days, he never gave up and never stopped walking despite having suffered a dislocated ankle. Through it all though, it's undeniable that Jhonattan was also very lucky with what had happened.

What if the dirty water he drank seriously contaminated him and made him incredibly ill from the inside out?

What if the wild pigs he had scared away by firing the shotgun at him did not run off and attacked him?

What if a venomous spider or snake had bitten him while he slept?

What if the jaguar he had caught sight of had seriously stalked him? With the empty shotgun, he would have been almost entirely defenseless against the predator had it elected to attack him. The fact the big cat never attacked him when he was such easy prey remained a mystery to Jhonattan after the incident.

There's no denying that Jhonattan was determined to make it out alive, that he always remained hopeful despite the overwhelming circumstances facing him, and that his knowledge of safe fruits and plants to eat helped him. But there's also no denying that he got extremely lucky as well, and that degree of luck doesn't happen to everyone who finds themselves stranded in the Amazon.

Like we said before: if you ever find yourself stranded in the Amazon, you are at the mercy of the jungle and its inhabitants. Jhonattan was at its mercy, and thankfully, he was allowed to live. But if you ever find yourself alone in the depths of the Amazon, it may not be so merciful to you.

CHAPTER ELEVEN

LOST ARROW

The true story of a Colorado hunter, whose name remains unreleased to this day, who survived after being impaled in the leg by another hunter's lost arrow. Using common sense, the hunter elected to stay in place and was able to contact rescuers to carry him to safety.

Our next story of survival takes us up into the mountains of Colorado. Like many states positioned among the Rockies in the western United States, Colorado is known for its rugged mountains, vast forests, and abundance of wildlife.

It's for this reason that the state is a major haven for hunters, attracting both hunters who are residents of the state and those who fly in from elsewhere in the country (or the world for that matter).

Many of these hunters who come to Colorado come during archery season. Hunting with a bow and arrow is very traditional and also more difficult than hunting with a rifle.

Archery hunting simply comes with a certain thrill and a challenge to it that hunting with a rifle, or a shotgun doesn't come with. This is precisely why there are many hunters who prefer to hunt with a bow.

However, archery hunters need to remember that there are many responsibilities that come with archery hunting, including certain responsibilities that don't exactly come with hunting with a rifle. One of those responsibilities is the necessity of, if possible, locating and retrieving any arrows you fire.

Let's say that you're an archery hunter in the woods. You spot a deer, take careful aim with your bow, and let your arrow fly…but your arrow misses. It's too easy to keep walking on without thinking twice about searching for the arrow that you just fired and missed with, but it's still something you need to do.

Why is this? Simple: that arrow could pose a threat to a future hunter who comes to that area. What if the missed arrow is sticking out of the ground with the pointed end sticking up, and another hunter comes stumbling through the brush and doesn't notice the arrow…only for it to be too late before they walk right into the path of the pointed end?

And while you may think that the odds of another hunter walking around in the woods running into and becoming impaled or injured with that arrow are extremely remote, the truth is it's still very much possible.

This is exactly what happened to one hunter who ventured out into Colorado's woods in October of 2022.

* * *

It was early October of 2022 and hunting season was in full swing in Colorado.

Routt County, located in northern Colorado, is a hunter's paradise. Deer, elk, and bear can be found in great abundance in Routt, and that's why the county attracts thousands of hunters to it each year. It's also this time of year when the Routt County Search and Rescue (RCSAR) needs to be on extra high alert.

One afternoon, the RCSAR team received an emergency SOS message from a hunter who had sent out the message on a radio beacon. The hunter had impaled himself with an arrow, and he was unable to walk out on his own. He dispatched his coordinates in the message.

The RCSAR team immediately got to work. They rode on ATVs and UTVs four miles north of Steamboat Springs, one of the local towns, and then hiked a further two and a half miles through the woods to reach the South Fork.

The terrain suddenly became a lot more unforgiving. The trees and brush became thick and difficult to walk through, and even when the RCSAR team managed to push themselves through that, they now arrived at a knee-deep marshy swamp.

But if they were to reach the hunter in time before he passed out (or worse), the team knew they had to push on. They pushed another mile and a half through the swamps, filled with cold and murky water, until they were able to reach the coordinates of the hunter.

Sure enough, the hunter was there. He was laying down on the ground and his leg was covered in blood, but he had wrapped a tourniquet around his thigh to help control the bleeding. In the time since sending his coordinates to the RCSAR team, he had removed the arrow from his leg…and as it turned out, he was perhaps incredibly lucky to have survived doing so.

"With penetrating injuries, it is never recommended to remove the object in the field." said the VP of RCSAR, Harry Sandler, in a statement after the incident. "It is best to let surgeons in the hospital perform this task. Leaving the object in reduces the chances of severe bleeding and additional tissue damage."

After speaking with the hunter, the RCSAR team was able to piece together what had happened. He had walked off trail through thick brush and failed to notice the arrow sticking out of the ground. He then walked straight into the path of the arrow, and the pointed edge punctured his skin and flesh and impaled him right above the knee.

The first thing he did after being wounded was to tie a tourniquet around his leg, and then he called in for help. This emergency rescue beacon was dangerously low on battery, so he sent in his coordinates to RCSAR before shutting the device off to conserve battery.

The team determined that carrying the hunter out was too dangerous considering his condition. They had just pushed their way through several miles of thick brush and knee-deep swamps, and the hunter walking through the swamp with an open leg wound carried a major risk of infection.

It was decided that the only way to get the hunter out was to carry him to a clearing where a helicopter could arrive to airlift him to safety. A twin-engine Bell-429 helicopter then arrived so he

The hunter, who elected to remain anonymous, was very lucky to be alive. But he was alive, and that is what mattered most.

* * *

Arrows that are left behind in the woods in this manner are referred to as 'lost arrows'...and they are a problem. This was the second incident in two years where RCSAR had to rescue a hunter who had impaled himself with such a lost arrow.

"The arrow was presumably released earlier in the archery hunting season," said RCSAR in a statement later. "This is RCSAR's second rescue involving a hunter walking into and becoming impaled by a lost arrow in the past two years."

And that's just in Routt County, Colorado. Think about the rest of the United States, and then think about the rest of the world. Lost arrows are a major problem and can be a major threat to hunters, hikers, and other people who go for a walk out in the woods.

It's also important that even though the hunter in this incident made a mistake in pulling the arrow out of his leg, he also did several things right that led to his rescue, and it's important to note what these things are.

First, he stayed calm and didn't allow panic to overwhelm him. After recognizing that he had been stabbed in the leg by the arrow, he laid down and tied a tourniquet around his thigh to prevent further loss of blood.

Then, he immediately contacted for help with his rescue beacon. Many hunters don't carry rescue beacons or communication devices when they are out in the woods, but this hunter was smart enough to. And since his beacon was low on battery life, he was wise to shut off to conserve the battery life in case help didn't arrive and he would need to use it again.

"Hunters should also always carry the ten essentials and be prepared for rapidly changing weather as is common this time of year in the Rockies," Sandler continued. "Regarding last week's hunter, having a PLB or satellite messenger likely saved this hunter's life as he was alone, immobile and in an extremely remote area with no cell service."

It's also important to note the extreme perseverance and dedication that the RCSAR team in this incident displayed to rescue the hunter. The hunter wasn't just stuck in a remote area of the Colorado woods, he was trapped in an area that was surrounded by extremely difficult terrain. But the RCSAR team who rescued him didn't let that stop them. They pushed their way through miles of dense woods and knee-deep swamps to find him.

Additionally, it's important for archery hunters to find and retrieve lost arrows if they can.

"While we know that it is not always feasible, bowhunters should make every effort possible to find a lost arrow," said Sandler.

Make retrieving any arrow or bolt you fire in the woods a part of your standard safety precautions. You don't know who'll be walking around in the woods next, who could walk right into that arrow and not realize it until it's too late.

CHAPTER TWELVE

BOW HUNTING FOR MOOSE...OR BLACK BEAR?

The story of Brent Prokulevich, who was bow hunting for moose in the woods of Ontario when he suddenly found himself confronted by a black bear instead. Only Brent's quick thinking enabled him to survive the attack.

Hunters routinely put themselves into environments where two primary kinds of big game animals exist: unaggressive animals (like elk or deer) that will usually run away at the first sight of a hunter, and then animals that are known to be more aggressive and could pose a bigger threat (such as bear, wolves, or mountain lion).

Encountering an aggressive bear in the wilderness is perhaps the last type of animal that any hunter would want to encounter. Bears are much larger than wolves or mountain lions, and they are surprisingly fast and agile as well. They have jaws that can crush bone, and massive claws that can tear deep into flesh.

Furthermore, bears are often difficult to stop. Pepper spray often doesn't cut it, and neither to big caliber firearms as well. There are countless stories of hunters who encounter an aggressive black bear or grizzly bear in the woods and will shoot the attacking bear multiple times in self-defense before the bear finally stops, if it even does stop.

Every hunter who goes into the forest to hunt should have three primary objectives: 1. To not get lost and know how to walk out, 2. To find and shoot the game animal that they're hunting, and 3. To avoid encountering a more aggressive animal along the way.

In the event that number three cannot be avoided, however, a hunter will have only one choice: to stand his ground and fight. But if that hunter has to stand his ground and fight against a bear, he will likely be in for one of the most life-threatening experiences he'll ever have.

This is exactly what happened to a hunter named Brent Prokulevich in September of 2011 in Western Ontario.

* * *

Brent Prokuleveich was a moose hunter. Moose are found aplenty in Ontario. While not particularly mountainous, Ontario is known for its sprawling woodlands and swamps, which is the perfect environment for moose. This is why Ontario is known as a moose hunter's paradise.

But Brent was also acutely aware of the dangers of encountering aggressive animals in the woods. Moose themselves are especially known for being more aggressive than deer or elk, especially during mating season or when a mother moose is defending her calf.

When Brent went moose hunting that day on September 26th of 2011, he fully expected that if he were going to have to defend himself against an aggressive animal that it would be a moose.

Little did he know that he would find himself up against an overly aggressive bear instead.

Brent flew into Chase Lake that day to meet with his friend Paul Patiuk and Paul's son, Kyle. Chase Lake is a part of the Woodland Caribou Provincial Park located in the far western part of the province. Covered in vast boreal forests, the park attracts thousands of outdoorsmen and women every year, including hunters.

Access to the park is only via canoe or plane, as it has over 1,200 miles of waterways that make access via cars impossible. The fact that the park is so remote is one reason why it has such a high population of moose, and that's why Brent fully expected to have a successful hunt this trip.

Paul and Kyle had already been hunting in the area for a few days, but to no avail. Nonetheless, they had been scouting the area very extensively and Paul had discovered an area with fresh moose sign that he believed would be a good spot for Brent to hunt.

The trio's plan was simple: Brent would hunt on his own on Sunday and Monday in this area that Paul had scouted out for him. Then on Tuesday, the trio would regroup and hunt together.

Brent knew full well the dangers of encountering an aggressive moose, but he also knew full well the dangers of encountering an aggressive bear. After all, where there are moose, there are usually bears too.

That's why after Brent landed and met with Paul and Kyle, he was sure to ask them if they had seen any signs of bears in the area. They told him that they had seen no bear sign in the area during the duration of their visit.

Brent arrived at the area Paul had scouted in a boat. Armed with a bow and arrows, he hunted that area all day Saturday, but he had the same luck Paul and Kyle had. While he was able to get a female moose to respond to a call he was using, he never saw a moose come into view. But there were definitely moose in the area, based on the fresh sign he was seeing and the cow moose who had responded to his call, so Brent was encouraged.

He decided to leave his moose scent rag in the area overnight. The idea was that the scent would fill the area and attract more moose into it for hopefully a successful hunt the next day.

Brent returned the next Monday to the boat. There was a thick fog in the air, and the wind had died down. This meant that his moose calls were able to carry over a longer distance, and the fog meant that hopefully moose would not be alerted to his presence visually.

Ninety minutes had passed of Brent making his moose calls. The fog was thick, and the air was still.

Suddenly, Brent heard movement in the trees about thirty yards away from him. Quickly, he set his moose call down and prepared his bow and arrow. He would have a clear shot when the moose emerged.

But it wasn't a moose that appeared out of the trees. The moment the animal appeared Brent knew exactly what it was: a black bear.

The moment the black bear emerged out of the trees, it looked straight ahead of itself and locked eyes with Brent.

That's when Brent's heart began pounding. He knew he was in danger. This bear was big, and it was making direct eye contact with him right now. And since it was only thirty yards away, it could close the gap and attack Brent quickly if it decided to charge.

"Get!" Brent yelled out at the bear. "Get! Get! Get!"

Brent hoped the bear would be skittish and run away at his hollering.

But the opposite happened.

The bear charged forward!

Brent fired an arrow at the bear and struck it in the chest.

But it did nothing to stop the ferocious animal and within seconds the bear was up on Brent before he could reload his bow with another arrow.

Instinctively, Brent raised his left arm to block the bear's blow. He went falling back over the ground with the full weight of the three-hundred-pound beast over him.

The bear's massive jaw locked over Brent's arm and his teeth sank deep into the flesh and bone of the arm, but because Brent's adrenaline was rushing so viciously, he felt no pain.

The bear released its jaws over Brent's arm, and then it went straight for his neck.

This one Brent felt. The bear's teeth sank into his neck and collar bone area. The pain was excruciating, and Brent yelled out in pain.

The bear was over him, its jaws were locked over the side of his neck, and the full weight of the animal was over him and pinning him to the ground. Brent's position was seemingly hopeless.

Brent thought about his seventeen-year-old son, Brady. Brent was a single father and the thought flashed into his mind then that if he were to die that day, Brady would have to live the rest of his life without a parent.

"I wasn't going to leave him to live by himself," Brent recalled when thinking about the incident after. "Something in me snapped. I'm not dying like this!"

* * *

Brent was already fighting back but at the moment he decided not to die. With his one good arm he attempted to reach for the hunting knife he carried on his belt, but he couldn't reach it.

Thinking fast, Brent reached for another arrow he carried on him instead. He then began stabbing the bear numerous times in its head and neck.

The bear released its grip over Brent's neck and began to pull away, but Brent continued stabbing the arrow, this time into the bear's chest.

It was then that Brent began to realize his first arrow had done its deadly work: the arrow had entered the bear's chest and exited out its abdomen, and the animal's entrails were now hanging out.

The bear finally broke completely away from Brent and backed up. Both Brent and the bear were in critical condition. Brent's left arm and the side of his neck and shoulder were torn apart from the bear's jaw, while the bear had sustained numerous punctures with its intestines hanging out from its abdomen.

Both man and beast were panting and breathing heavily, both knowing that this moment may be their last. The two made eye contact again, but this time, neither made another attack.

Finally, the bear turned around and walked for around fifteen yards before collapsing from its wounds and exhaustion.

Brent knew the bear would slowly die, but he wanted to put another round into his bow to finish off the animal and give it a quick death. To this dismay, he found that his bow was destroyed beyond use from his struggle with the animal.

The only thing he could do was get up and walk out and leave the bear to die on its own.

Brent staggered his way back down to the boat, suffering an egregious loss of blood. He took off in the boat and headed back into camp. Even though his companions were not there, to Brent's pleasant surprise, a plane came landing at the camp.

The pilot's name was Kevin, and Brent brought up the boat to shore and ran up to him to tell him what had happened. He left a note for Paul and Kyle, and then he boarded the plane with Kevin to take off to a hospital, where they arrived thirty minutes later.

Brent walked right up to the front desk in the hospital and said, "I've been attacked by a bear."

* * *

Brent did what few hunters have ever managed to do. He fought a bear with his bare hands…and won.

But Brent was extremely lucky. When the doctors got to work at repairing his torn flesh, they told him the bear's neck and shoulder bite was only half an inch from puncturing his lung and hitting his spinal cord. This would have surely resulted in death as it would have paralyzed Brent on the spot and made it extremely difficult for him to breathe.

It was definitely a bit of luck that enabled Brent to survive, but what also helped him was his quick thinking and determination to make it out alive. He fought valiantly back against the bear rather than let it rip him to shreds, first by shooting the bear with the first arrow and then by stabbing it repeatedly with his second arrow.

Had Brent not fought back as furiously as he did, it's an absolute certainty that he and not the bear would have been the one to die that day.

CHAPTER THIRTEEN

UPSIDE DOWN

The story of a Texas hunter who found himself suspended in the air and hanging upside down out of his tree stand. Even so, he was able to successfully contact help to come to his rescue.

Like we've talked about earlier in this book, a tree stand can be a great asset for a hunter. But it can also be a serious liability.

That's because when positioned strategically in an area known to be teeming with game, a tree stand can give a hunter the perfect vantage point upon which to make an ambush.

But if you're not too careful, it's very possible to fall out of your tree stand and break a bone or two…or, as we'll soon see, to get caught in the tree stand and find yourself hanging upside down.

In November of 2022, first responders in Spurger, Texas received a call from a desperate deer hunter who was saying that this was exactly what had happened to him: he was hanging upside down eighteen feet up from his climbing tree stand.

He was unable to climb back into the stand, and if attempted to cut himself loose with a knife, he would risk potentially fatal injury dropping all the way to the bottom.

* * *

Spurger is a town located in eastern Texas. The area is surrounded by dense woodland that is perfect for deer hunters, and hunters with their tree stands are a common presence in the Spurger area. This time of the year, it was bow hunting season.

At approximately 4:30 PM, the Sheriff's Office received a call from the hunter who dialed 911. The hunter explained that he was suspended in the air after attempting to climb out of his tree stand, and that he was hanging on by his boot.

The hunter had first attempted to call another hunter he knew in the area, but when this was unsuccessful, he elected to call 911 instead.

The Sheriff's Department then contacted the Spurger Volunteer Fire Department and the Texas Parks and Wildlife to assist in the rescue.

One hour later, the entire team of rescuers reached the site of the dangling hunter. Somehow miraculously, he was still hanging on by his boot and had never fallen.

The rescuers pulled up with a brush truck that belonged to the city and positioned it under the hunter. They then used ladders to ascend to the hunter's position and they were able to cut him free and lower him into the brush truck.

"He was high off the ground, with his right foot wedged in the framework of his climbing stand," LeBlanc said. "He'd been hanging long enough that his fluids and blood were rushing to his head. He's lucky his phone didn't hit the ground."

The hunter elected to remain anonymous, because he didn't want his name to be released to the public. He knew that if his name went out, he would receive lifelong mockery from the incident.

"They saved my life," the anonymous hunter would later say, referring to the first responders. "I was eighteen feet up, and my ankle was the only thing that was holding me up. I held my phone in my mouth. I knew if I dropped this, I'd die."

Thankfully, the hunter did not require any medical attention, but an ambulance was on standby just in case he did. He was also lucky that he had suffered no severe injury to his foot or ankle.

This is why it's vitally important for hunters to take all available safety precautions when using a tree stand. One of those precautions is to always use a safety harness. This particular hunter had failed to do so, and if he wasn't lucky enough for his boot to have caught onto the tree stand, he would have fallen nearly twenty feet to the ground and potentially sustained a severe injury such as a leg fracture, or worse, a spinal injury that could have paralyzed him on the spot.

The hunter was also extremely lucky that his phone did not slip out of his pocket and fall out of reach. If it did, he would have been unable to have contacted anyone for help, Unable to slip out of his boot or cut himself free, he would have been suspended there for several more hours if not days and would have had to have waited for another hunter or person to come walking along (which wasn't a certainty).

Always practice extreme vigilance when using a tree stand. Always wear a safety harness, make sure that your stand is secured firmly to the tree, and be extremely slow and deliberate in your movements getting in and out of the stand.

That hunter was lucky for the reasons explained above, but if you don't practice the necessary precautions, you might not be so lucky yourself.

CONCLUSION

In this book, we've traveled from the mountains of Alaska to the forests of Canada to the backwoods of the American South to the frigid lakes of Minnesota to the oceans off the coast of Florida and to the depths of the Amazon Rainforest.

But through all of these stories of hunters who survived harrowing life-threatening experiences all over the world, there remains one common thread that unites all of them: stay calm and think carefully about what you need to do to survive.

Every single one of these hunters found themselves locked in these difficult circumstances, whether it be by their own mistakes or by chance, but every single one of them stayed calm and thought carefully about what they needed to do to survive.

If you're a hunter yourself, the number one most important thing to remember is to always be prepared when you venture out into the wilderness. Always carry food, water, a survival blanket, a knife, fire-starting devices, a water filter, a first aid kit, and a GPS or a compass with you at the bare minimum. Just these items alone will always make your survival efforts much easier.

The second most important thing to remember is to never give up and follow the lead from each of the subjects of the story we've covered here today. Stay calm and think carefully about your circumstances and what you need to do. Not one of the hunters that we have covered in this book ever gave up hope that they would make it out alive.

Hopefully, you'll never find yourself in a predicament in the woods on a future hunting trip that will turn into the kind of survival story we've covered in this book!

But if you ever do, think back on these stories, and reflect on the lessons that you can learn from them. Every single one of the hunters in this story did a few things right to ensure their survival, and that's why the lessons from these stories can be truly invaluable to you.

Made in the USA
Las Vegas, NV
15 November 2023